YES YOU CAN
(AND YOU SHOULD!)
READ
THE KING JAMES BIBLE

DAVID W. DANIELS

Includes material researched and presented on our YouTube channel, youtube.com/c/chicktracts, namely from:
The Hardest Passage in the KJV?
The Superiority of the King James Bible
How To Get Great Faith

For a list of bookstores outside of the USA,
call (909) 987-0771, or visit www.chick.com/bookstores

Copyright © 2019 David W. Daniels

Published by:
CHICK PUBLICATIONS
PO Box 3500, Ontario, Calif. 91761-1019 USA
Tel: (909) 987-0771
Fax: (909) 941-8128
Web: www.chick.com
Email: postmaster@chick.com

First Printing

Printed in the United States of America

All rights reserved. No part of this book may be reproduced, stored in a retrieval system or transmitted in any form or by any means (electronic, mechanical, photocopying, recording or otherwise) without permission in writing from the copyright owner.

ISBN: 978-0-75891-3098

Annotated Table of Contents

- **Finally, an Everyman's Bible** 9

    Until about 1600, most of the copies of the Bible were in the hands of the educated and scholars. No one Bible was commonly used by the general public. King James used his authority to commission a group of world-class scholars to make such a Bible. His authorized version was both written in a classic English worthy of the word of God, and simple enough for the plowboy to read and understand.

Part I – Is the King James Too Hard? 16

    We learn new concepts every day. So, why do people complain that the King James is "too hard," because it contains some less-common words?

- **Anything you don't already know can seem hard** 18

    Reading the Bible isn't anywhere near as difficult as studying for a degree or learning stonemasonry. All you need to do is give God your time and a little bit of effort.

- **Context Is The Key To Understanding God's Words** 19

    Words have different meanings that are determined by context. And if you pay attention, you will generally be able to understand which meaning is correct in that context.

- **What About All that Punctuation?** 20

  The King James Bible is very clear about sentence structure. What we have is a simple way to understand what God said if we slow down, take our time, and pay attention to every word.

- **Rhythm and Cadence** 21

  If you have trouble reading a word or phrase quickly, take a breath, and read it more slowly. When you do, you'll be able to hear it. When you hear it, it will add to your understanding. If you read modern versions, you will find that the Bible often loses this memorable cadence.

- **2nd Corinthians 6:11-13** 22

  The unusual language that is used here was specially chosen by the translators to convey exactly the same ideas Paul expressed in Greek. If you want accuracy, this is what Paul wrote. The King James Bible makes clear to us that Paul felt strong emotions. It doesn't hide the emotional words under a layer of "scholarliness." It really is "the people's Bible." God intended for common folk to grab hold of His holy words and have them affect them on a daily and very personal basis.

PART 2 – WHY YOU SHOULD READ THE KING JAMES BIBLE 28

  This is the only English Bible that is a true and reliable translation, that faithfully passes down God's preserved words.

- A True and Reliable Translation.................. 28

    The King James Bible was translated by men whose agenda was to give the exact English meaning of the Greek or Hebrew originals, without injecting their personal biases. Most other modern versions are not based on the reliable copies of the originals used for the KJV. They are the product of unreliable manuscripts containing man's opinions.

- A Faithfully Passed-Down Bible.................. 30

    If Jesus' words shall not pass away, as He promised, then there must be some place where they can be found. Jesus did not want His truths to be secret, or hidden. He wanted them to be out in the open, for all to see.

- The King James Bible Provides a Checklist.......... 31

    If the Ruler of the universe has given you the secret to happiness, joy and fulfillment in this life, and rewards and blessings in the next, wouldn't you want to grab that Book and learn it, and live it, and be blessed? I would. And I do. And you can, too. Just be sure to have the RIGHT checklist.

Part 3 – The Superiority of the King James Bible 36

    What has the King James Bible done for the world? It has changed lives. The more we have learned, the more reasons we have today to talk about the superiority of the King James Bible.

- What has the King James Bible done for the world?... 37
- It Brought Me Conviction And Boldness............ 45
- It Brought Me Doctrinal Clarity................... 46
- It Rescued Me From The Confusion In Bible College And Seminary 57
- Its Words Have Power........................... 58
- Its History Shows That God Had A Plan............ 71

Part 4 – Here's How.....................79

- A 30-Day Challenge............................ 79

    As the preceding chapters illustrate, the King James is not too hard to read. But it does take some practice to get started. I challenge you to read it out loud each day for 30 days.

- The 5-Ribbon Plan............................ 80

    There are five easy sections to our Bible. If we read just a bit from each section every day, we will start learning about our God and what He wants us to know.

- The Proverbs Reading Plan..................... 84

    Every month has no more than 31 days. Proverbs has 31 chapters. At any time, we can look at the calendar and see which day it is. Then we can grab that chapter of Proverbs and start reading. It's that simple!

Appendix 85

- The King James Bible Companion 85
- Charts 108
    1. Hebrew Calendar 108
    2. Hebrew Feast Days 110
    3. Hebrew Time 112
    4. Hebrew Weights 114
    5. Biblical Money 116
    6. Biblical Measures 117
        a. Length 117
        b. Dry Measure 118
        c. Liquid Measure 119
- The Bible's Internal Timeline 120

Finally, an Everyman's Bible

In 1611, an amazing thing happened: God's words, Old and New Testaments, were published in a single-language book that *everyone* could read and learn from. It was written in language that exalts God, and yet was not too complex for the common Christian. It revolutionized the English language, and in fact was the basis for Modern English. Critics, and even atheists, have commended its production. It not only read accurately, it read *well*. It lifted the spirit, tugged at the heart and exalted the Lord Jesus Christ.

That was then. This is now. People are saying, "The King James was alright for the 17th century, but it's too old and too difficult for the 21st century." Is it?

Not at all! God's precepts are from everlasting, He changes not. So the content is for us today. And the wording? When writing *The King James Bible Companion,* I was able to identify only about 600 words not familiar to the average 5th grader. When that 5th grader has already learned 8,000+ words, learning a few hundred more is a piece of cake. (The King James has a vocabulary of only about 8,000 root words.)

The King James Bible was devised by God. It was the visible manifestation of God keeping His promise to preserve His holy words. And do you think He knew what would happen to the English language, and planned His book to stand the tests of time? Absolutely! Even when the most doubt-ridden scholars criticize this holy Book, a ten-year-old raised with this Bible can answer most of the questions the scholar would raise. **When you have God's Book, you have God's answers.** They're all there and He changes "not". All we have to do is learn to find and read them.

The first time you read through the Bible, it will be like flying around in a space capsule. The next time like flying at 30,000 feet. You'll see the mountains and rivers. The next time like flying in a propeller plane. You'll have to avoid mountains and fly away from storms. The next time like a helicopter. You'll recognize people, events, places, buildings, and see people fairly clearly. The next time like you're staying to walk and talk with the people. You will see what they see and hear what they hear.

Now God can land the capsule or plane or helicopter at any time, and give you glimpses. That's because you are dealing with the living God. And these are His words. This is His Book. But however it works out for you, each time you read will always be new, when you approach His words with a heart open to Him.

The ten-year-old has the advantage, frankly, because he or she started with *faith in God's words.* That is the right starting point. And if that child has been saved by faith in the shed blood of Jesus, he or she has a treasure-trove of information available because he or she has also received the Holy Ghost, who has promised to enlighten the seeker. God Himself, has promised to dispense wisdom to whoever is desperate enough to beg Him for it (See Proverbs 2:1-6; James 1:5).

But what about all those changes in the English language? Languages are always changing. Terms that are totally acceptable in one decade, sound dated and "uncool" in the next.

Language is a moving target. Any attempt to pin it down is futile. But God had a plan to guarantee **permanent accuracy** for His words. He decided to set up circumstances where He could get His words into a classic English that English speakers of all time could read. That way, it wasn't necessary to keep up with the ever-changing meanings and connotations. It was only necessary to keep on reading them.

His original wording in the 1611 KJV was so well done that it became the **standard** for commerce, religion, and education vocabularies wherever anyone spoke English. And it informed a great deal of the Oxford Unabridged English Dictionary. Many definitions were illustrated by verses from the King James! The same is true of the 1828 Noah Webster's American English Dictionary.

God's plan was to make an eternal standard version in English that we could all easily learn to read throughout the centuries, during which English was the international language. Prior to English, He used Hebrew, Greek and Latin, the foundation languages of the final English Bible.

It is beginning to look like English may be the final end-time language. Jesus said, "And this gospel of the kingdom shall be preached in all the world for a witness unto all nations; and then shall the end come." (Matthew 24:14). English has been the foundational, common, international language so many have used to create the other Bible translations. God seems to be using English-speakers to fulfill that prophecy. If the end is near, as so many believe, the Classic English of the King James could well be the last of the great, world-class base languages used to spread God's preserved words.

In God's providence (providing for our needs), He made choices. He chose to reveal Himself in Hebrew and Greek. So any conversations or writings that were in other languages were translated into Hebrew in the Old Testament and later Greek in the New Testament. He chose to have those words, in turn, translated into other languages. But at the advent of mass-printing, He chose a world language for a single-language Bible that was correct. He chose English, knowing in advance that it would become the next world language. And it is. I believe history is showing us that English is the language of the End Times. It is the Last-Days language. It is largely from English that the versions have sprung. So it is from the King James Bible and preserved Greek and Hebrew that all languages need their Bibles translated. I want all nations to have God's words in their language. But right now, the Devil has been hard at work, getting doubting words translated instead, through Vatican-approved alliances, as I proved in ***Why They Changed the Bible: One World Bible for One World Religion.***

The Devil didn't like this Book of God's words in English. He wanted to destroy it any way he could. In other countries, after the Reformation, Satan got largely Roman Catholic leadership to run the schools (often by Jesuits), and either change the meaning of the words to Catholic-favoring meanings, or to eliminate the use of certain words altogether.

Unlike the other countries, by God's grace, England stood strong. The Devil was unable to destroy the Bible. However, when he got people to switch Bibles starting in the late 1800s, he did get people to stop using *some* of the words.

But here's what is exciting. Satan could never get all the Christians on his bandwagon. There were always the King James literalists, who trusted every word and refused to let go of them. And so many educated people, Christian and non-Christian alike, kept using the vocabulary of the King James, so it never completely left the English language.

That brings us to where we are today. A growing number of people are discovering the emptiness in the modern Bibles.

People see how other Bibles lower Christ and destroy the Godhead. They raise doubts about salvation by faith instead of works. And they feed doubts about the history and the words of God's Son, Jesus Himself. The resulting doubts are suspiciously like a certain snake's question: "Yea, hath God said?"

That emptiness is not filled by another "new" or "improved" version. It's a God-shaped vacuum, and it can only be filled by His holy words. Not 95%, not 99%, but 100% the words of God. That's what changes lives, because it has the hand of God on it.

Many people thought Solomon's temple was less than what God wanted, because it wasn't the same as the tabernacle in the wilderness. I heard that taught a number of times. But you know how you can read the Bible over and over, and suddenly you notice something that you missed before? Look at this. The Bible describes the elements that were prepared for the temple. It's a section many people skip over. But note these words:

"Then David gave to Solomon his son **the pattern…**"
"…And **the pattern of all that he had by the spirit…**" (1 Chronicles 28:11-12)

And after David described all the features of the temple and purchased the materials to make it, he said to Solomon:

"All *this, said David*, the LORD made me understand in writing **by *his* hand upon me**, *even* **all the works of this pattern**" (1 Chronicles 28:19).

God, by inspiration, wrote through David (made him understand in writing) all parts of that coming temple. Solomon didn't have to improvise on *anything*. It was all laid out. The Lord knew what Solomon was going to need. So in His providence He gave David the "pattern," just as God showed Moses the "pattern" of the tabernacle (Exodus 25:9, 40; Numbers 8:4). *God left nothing to chance.*

He did the same in giving us the Bible that we call "The King James Bible." **He left nothing to chance.** His hand was all over that Bible, above every other English book.

Do you think that people writing the Bible books said while they were writing them, "I think I shall write inspired words of God for all ages"? Of course not! They were totally in the dark as to God's plan. **But God wasn't.** He picked and chose and wrote by inspiration through whomever He desired.

Let's bring that into the present. The Devil had some early successes, getting people to remove words, phrases and verses from Bible texts (like Acts 8:37 and 1 John 5:7). But God still inspired those words, and He wanted them back in his Bible, available to all for the end times. During the 1500s, He got His people to put those words back into the text. Do you think the scholars knew God was doing that through them? Of course not! They were, as far as they knew, just doing their job, trying to do their best work.

God is the One who compiled the text. And God had a plan. Isn't that exciting! And what convinced me was the fruit. I like to say, "The fruit proves the root." The fruit of reading and trusting the King James Bible is more faith in God, whether in believing the Bible events to be true, or in believing that God will get them through their human difficulties and human frailties. The King James Bible fulfills Romans 1:17:

"For therein is the righteousness of God revealed from faith to faith: as it is written, The just shall live by faith."

I have never had my faith boosted as when I started reading the King James Bible. And all I am going to share in this book has been proved true in my own walk with God. And "the proof of the pudding is in the eating," as the saying goes. I have friends who came to the King James cold turkey, with no prior experience, who followed the simple suggestions and ideas in this book. Now they are well on their way to being the godly type of Bible scholars —believers who know, trust, and act on what His Bible says. I have been amazed to see the transformation.

You are one step away from that same transformation. Even if you have read for years, there are probably some questions you may have had that will be answered. Or, you may have had some difficulties in reading the King James Bible over the years. And you are now ready to surmount those difficulties with the simple principles found in this book. Or, you may just be looking for a different way of reading and understanding the Bible than you have used previously. I hope the stories I tell, and the lessons weaved within them, will give you the stepping-stones you need to be a major Bible-reading Bible-believer.

But how do we begin? Yes, the secrets of God are readily available, but how do we get into those pages to see them? This book offers a simple method of Bible reading, and even gives a kick-start by including the entire King James Bible Companion, a dictionary of over 600 lesser-used words and their first occurrence, in the back. And I've added on Biblical Weights and Measures, as well as the Feast Days of the Bible, and how to recognize them in your King James.

So find a comfortable place, relax, and let me show you a world you knew existed, but wanted to enter: a world where the words of God were not only easy to understand with a little practice, but also were powerful and life-changing words.

God bless you as you proceed.

Part 1 – Is The King James Too Hard?

By 1980, when I came to read the Bible for the first time as a repentant believer, I had three Bibles in my possession. My main one was a giant Family Tree Bible King James. The newest one was an occultic Lamsa Bible, supposedly translated from an Aramaic text. Ironically, I bought both of them in different Religious Science churches, not a Christian bookstore.

I also still had my first King James Bible. I received that as a gift from a bishop, when I visited the Los Angeles Mormon Temple with other deacons to do baptisms for the dead!

I no longer had my very first Bible. It was a Red Revised Standard Version. I received it at a special Sunday service at my grandparents' Congregational church. I never read it, but I kept it for many years in a prominent place by itself.

So in my short lifetime I had owned a Revised Standard Version Bible, two King James Bibles, and an occultic Lamsa Bible.

I got my Bibles from the most interesting places: a liberal church, a cult, and an occultic group!

But whenever I read the King James Bible, I never worried about whether or not I could understand it.

I'm with my brother, holding my brand-new red Revised Standard Bible.

That thought never entered my mind. I just read it. I didn't know all the words, but whenever I came across a word I didn't know, I looked it up in a dictionary, in the glossary in the back, or just kept reading.

I could tell that the Lamsa Bible was *a* Bible and so was the Revised Standard (they said "Bible"), but the King James was *the* Bible. I didn't worry about how hard it might be. I simply learned whatever I needed to, in order to understand what I was reading.

All you need to read the King James Bible is a willingness to learn, like with any other Bible. I wrote the ***King James Bible Companion*** (included, with extras, in the back of this book) so people could learn the words as they went along and read them. But you can use a dictionary as well. Many people have them on their phones now. The information is not hard to find.

My wife and I came to faith in the King James when our kids were 9, 6, 5, 3 and 1, so most of our children learned to read with the King James Bible. They didn't find it any more difficult than any other book they read. To them, a new word was just another new word, whether it was "kingdom" or "leasing". They asked about the definitions, learned the answers and grew to understand as they went.

None of us lives in a vacuum. We're surrounded by people and resources that have information we haven't yet encountered, and we learn new concepts every day. And yet it is common to hear people complain that the King James is "too hard," because it contains some less-common words. Ironically, I hear that more from professors and teachers than from common folk.

Anything You Don't Already Know Can Seem Hard.

Anything can be too hard when you don't know it, but *nothing* is too hard once you've learned it.

Proverbs 14:6 says: "A scorner seeketh wisdom, and findeth it not: but knowledge is easy unto him that understandeth."

You cannot be a scorner and learn wisdom. But if you are open, you can build upon what you know and ascend to new heights of understanding.

This principle applies to any discipline. If you want to get a degree in any subject, there are new concepts you're going to have to learn about, and you will learn new words to describe those concepts. Perhaps you will even learn to use familiar words in unfamiliar ways. Well, guess what? People who have not studied the subject that you have, will be unfamiliar with that vocabulary.

If a person becomes an apprentice to become a stonemason, he will have to learn all sorts of techniques and skills, and they will all have names that people unfamiliar with stonemasonry won't know.

A student of any subject will most likely have to learn new terms in order to understand and communicate it to others, and to work efficiently in that discipline.

But reading the Bible isn't anywhere near as difficult as studying for a degree or learning stonemasonry. All you need to do is give God your time and a little bit of effort. If you start as I did, in Genesis and Matthew, and just work your way through the Old Testament and the New Testament, you will gain a progressive understanding of what the words mean and how they are used.

There are not as many unfamiliar words in the King James

Bible as you may think. Some of the words that appear to be more complex in the King James Bible are actually shorter words that you already know, stuck together to make longer words. Some common examples are words like "therein", "howbeit," "howsoever" and "moreover". You learn these as you go, because the sentences where you find them tell you what they mean.

The meaning of any word can generally be understood by its context. Read the entire verse or sentence. Then look at the words before and after a new word. They will help you understand it and how it is used.

Context Is The Key
To Understanding God's Words.

Many preachers and teachers misinterpret God's words because they ignore the context and instead search for hidden meanings in Hebrew, Greek or Aramaic. They take an English word, look it up in the original language using a lexicon or dictionary, find some obscure place where that word was used in an unusual way, and say, "That's part of its meaning in the Bible." No, it's not. That's just how the word was used in *that* context.

If I talk about *my* foot, you know I'm talking about the appendage at the bottom of my leg. But if I talk about the foot *of a mountain*, I'm not talking about something that has toes. There are no cuticles on the foot of the mountain. The foot of a mountain has a different meaning. Why? Because it's part of a mountain, not a man.

Words have different meanings that are determined by context. And if you pay attention, you will generally be able to understand which meaning is correct in that context.

What About All That Punctuation?

Why are all those semi-colons, colons, and periods in the King James? You can treat each one of them as a little stop sign. Take your time when you read and pause a moment at each one.

The King James Bible was made with the clear intention that it be read aloud in churches. Ministers would read it phrase by phrase, because the room had a natural echo. As a result, everyone could follow the clear, beautiful and memorable language. There's a good reason why the King James Bible was made that way. Try reading it aloud to yourself or to whoever is around. As you read it out loud to yourself, you'll be amazed at how much you understand, and how much more you get out of it.

The King James Bible is very clear about sentence structure. What we have in front of us is a simple way to understand what God said if we slow down, take our time, and pay attention **to every word**. If we skip words, we will miss things. God didn't waste His time putting all those words in the text. Every word means something.

Technical Stuff: Colons and Semicolons

A **colon** (:) establishes a hierarchy within a sentence. The clause (semi-sentence) after the colon further defines the principle or idea of the phrase or clause before the colon.

A **semicolon** (;) separates what are pretty much equal-level ideas. But the semicolon makes two sentences into one, so the second part (after the semicolon) further describes the same idea, but without all of the nouns and verbs from the first part.

Here is an example. This verse has both a colon and a semicolon:

> **Psalm 2:7** I will declare the decree: the LORD hath said unto me, Thou *art* my Son; this day have I begotten thee.

Everything after the colon ***describes*** the decree [the subject]. The two statements, before and after the semicolon, are ***equally important parts*** of that decree.

RHYTHM AND CADENCE

In my book, ***Look What's Missing,*** I showed how modern scholars have chosen to take things out of their Bibles. But when they took out those things, remember: they were removing God's words. As a result, they made the Bible lose a lot of its power, to say nothing of the key doctrines that were affected.

One day, my wife Deborah and I were at a funeral service. The pastor was speaking, and he was citing a scripture from a modern version. Right in the middle he paused, because he was trying to focus on all of us, and forgot the words in the version he was reading. Then he picked up again, easily quoting the rest of the verse from memory —from the King James Bible!

The King James words overpowered whatever modern version he had been reading. I have seen this in churches time and again. Perhaps you have, too.

The King James is so powerful that when other versions rub off, it's still there. You know why? Because it's ***memorable***. It's rhythmic. It was written so that you can feel it. It was written so that you can hear the words and they can echo back to you.

Try reading Exodus 32:27 aloud: *"And he said unto them,*

Thus saith the Lord God of Israel, Put every man his sword by his side, and go in and out from gate to gate throughout the camp, and slay every man his brother, and every man his companion, and every man his neighbor."

That sounds terrifying, but it's written in such a way that you don't have to drone on and on. Everything is written with rhythm, everything has a cadence. You can hear it just by regular reading, observing the punctuation and pausing at the pauses. The text doesn't even have to be poetic. It's rhythmic. If we don't rush, the meanings flow right into us.

If you have trouble reading a word or phrase quickly, take a breath, and read it more slowly. When you do, you'll be able to hear it. When you hear it, it will add to your understanding. If you read modern versions, you will find that the Bible often loses this memorable cadence.

2ND CORINTHIANS 6:11-13

Parts of the King James can seem confusing the first time you read them. An example that has been often cited by critics, including one of my professors at Fuller Seminary, is 2nd Corinthians 6:11-13.

But the unusual language that is used here was specially chosen by the translators to convey exactly the same ideas Paul expressed in Greek. If you take the time to learn the meanings of a couple of the English words used in the King James, you will gain a deeper appreciation of what is being said in this passage. Let's take a look at 2nd Corinthians 6:11-13:

(11) O ye Corinthians, our mouth is open unto you, our heart is enlarged. (12) Ye are not straitened in us, but ye are straitened in your own bowels. (13) Now for a recompence in the same, (I speak as unto my children,) be ye also enlarged.

It's clear that verse 11 is not talking about hearts that have increased in size, because then they'd have to have an operation or something. That wouldn't fit the context of the passage very well! Yet this is exactly the expression Paul uses in Greek. He has to be saying something that goes together with "our mouth is open unto you." Once again, context is our friend.

Paul has been talking in this vein all through this chapter: "Look, we're not trying to lift ourselves up above you. We really do care. Look what we've gone through for you."

He mentions all the stripes, and the imprisonments, the floggings, everything that's happened. "We... beseech you... receive not the grace of God in vain," it starts out in Chapter 6. Then he says, "O ye Corinthians, our mouth is open unto you, our heart is enlarged. Ye are not straitened…"

"Straiten," like the Straits of Magellan, means "to narrow, or tighten up." What happens when you feel your insides tightened up inside you? It makes it hard to think about others and their feelings. Try it. You think about yourself and your own feelings. I've had that feeling before. I bet you have, too.

Paul means, "We're not closed off to you. We're not straitened inside. You don't make us feel that tight feeling inside. We're open and enlarged toward you, not closed off." "Enlarged" is the opposite of "straitened."

Then it says, "... but ye are straitened in your own bowels." Which means, "You guys are the ones who are holding back from us. You are the guys who are feeling all tightened up inside. See, these words are emotion words. "Bowels" means your insides and "straitened" means tightened up. When you feel tightened up, you're feeling stingy or closed off. You're not feeling good about somebody else. You're certainly not going to open your heart to him or her.

"Now for a recompense in the same, (I speak as unto my children,) be ye also enlarged." Recompense is a response in a similar manner. Loosen up yourselves toward us, in the same way. We're loosened up for you and our hearts are enlarged. In other words, open up your heart to us. We're opening up our hearts to you.

Modern Bible scholars act like they fixed the passage by taking all the emotion out. It seems like they can think, but they can't *feel*. When they choose unemotional words, they miss something important that God wants us to know. And what it says in the King James is what it says in Greek. If you want accuracy, this is what Paul wrote. It says our mouth is open, our heart is enlarged. You are not straitened in us, you are straitened in your own bowels. That's exactly what Paul was writing under inspiration of God.

Are the other versions going to talk in generalities, or will they convey the feeling behind the meaning? Let's see. Here's 2 Corinthians 6:11-13 in the NRSV. "We have spoken frankly to you Corinthians; our heart is wide open to you. There is no restriction in our affections, but only in yours. In return, I speak as to children, open wide your hearts also."

That's analytical, not emotional. It sounds as dry as a doctor diagnosing postnasal drip.

It's close. But it's not what Paul said. We're talking a physical feeling. A restriction, a tightness inside your gut, not a restriction in your affections. That's a metaphorical paraphrase, but it's not what Paul wrote. If you want to know what Paul wrote, he wrote what it says right here in the literal translation, the King James.

If you learn a few words and read out loud a phrase at a

time, and feel what it feels like inside you, you'll understand exactly what he's saying.

What a feeling letter! Paul keeps stepping up the emotional context of the letter, until he says something like, "Look, I'm just going to jump into the highest level of exaggeration now: I'm going to boast about myself." His heart's just ripping apart because the Corinthian Christians accepted these false apostles who are taking advantage of the Corinthians, putting down the real apostles. All the while they are claiming they're sent from Peter, James, and John. Paul's really hurting over this.

The bottom line is this: The King James Bible makes clear to us that Paul felt strong emotions. It doesn't hide the emotional words under a layer of "scholarliness." It really is "the people's Bible." God intended for common folk to grab hold of His holy words and have them affect them on a daily and very personal basis.

The "big lie" is the story that the King James Bible is just some old book in outdated language. The truth is God picked words, in Hebrew and Greek, to communicate His purpose for His people. It was not made for priests. It was made for common folk.

Even when the Hebrews were gone for over a generation in the Babylonian Captivity, those words from God were not changed. Nehemiah 8 shows us that God instead moved His educated believers to help the common folk to understand those same words. The scholars didn't get to change them.

Fast-forward 2,000 years to the 1500s. God, again, started moving a people to seek out His words. And though they had been scattered all over the world, He superintended their being brought together again. It doesn't matter whether the writers fully knew what God was doing through them. God knew. He would fulfill His promises to preserve His own inspired words.

In 1604, God did something spectacular: He gathered a committee of believers from two opposing viewpoints and got them to agree on every single verse of 1,189 chapters of the Bible. And that took away personal bias and denominational distinctives from the text. The resulting Book is what is now known as the King James Bible.

Those King James translators gave God's words to us in English words that matched the Greek wording and meaning. This preserved the emotions that Paul and others were feeling when they wrote the Greek. And it transferred the meaning of the Greek and Hebrew into one single language: modern English.

God had a plan. God enacted the plan. And we benefit from that plan: God's holy and preserved words translated into English.

When we pick up a King James Bible, we should have a reverent heart. These are God's words in our hands. When we read, we need to ask the Lord of the universe to help us understand His words by His Holy Spirit. His promise is that if we trust Him and meditate on His words, He will help us understand them.

1 John 2:27 But the anointing which ye have received of him abideth in you, and ye need not that any man teach you: but as the same anointing teacheth you of all things, and is truth, and is no lie, and even as it hath taught you, ye shall abide in him.

Psalm 19:7 The law of the LORD *is* perfect, converting the soul: the testimony of the LORD *is* sure, making wise the simple.

Psalm 119:99 I have more understanding than all my teachers: for thy testimonies *are* my meditation.

No scholar on earth can teach you like God can. Trust no substitutes. No matter who tells you that you cannot understand the Bible, God says you can. That's why He gave us the Bible in the first place. But we must come to him in faith and ask for His help. He will take it from there.

PART 2 – WHY YOU *SHOULD* READ THE KING JAMES BIBLE

In Part 1 you learned that the King James Bible is not really that hard to read. Like every other serious book, you need to put in a little work to understand the words. But with an ordinary Webster's Dictionary and *The King James Bible Companion,* the average 5th grader will have no difficulty deciphering the words.

However, the other objection we face when we attempt to read the King James in public is that we should NOT read it.

Some say it has antiquated or outdated language. Others claim it was made from lesser-quality manuscripts. Or how about these? "My pastor uses something else." "My friends think I am [fill in the blank]." Or maybe you've heard some other reason. So, how do I deal with that?

Without getting into all the details, the simple answer is: "*This is the only English Bible that is a true and reliable translation, that faithfully passes down God's preserved words.*"

A TRUE AND RELIABLE TRANSLATION

The King James Bible was translated by men whose agenda was to give the exact English meaning of the Greek or Hebrew originals, without injecting their personal biases. Amazingly, Puritans and members of the Church of England (who disagreed on almost every denominational issue) had to come together and agree on every verse of 1,189 chapters of the Bible, going over the text no less than 14 times. God used that process to take out personal and denominational bias. What was left was a true translation, stripped of personal opinions or interpretations.

Most other modern versions are not based on the reliable copies of the originals used for the KJV. They are the product of unreliable manuscripts containing man's opinions. I tell about this in ***Look What's Missing*** and ***Did the Catholic Church Give Us the Bible?***

Although most modern Bibles are called "translations," they are really more like commentaries, colored by the personal interpretations or preferences of the "translators." God said to Moses:

"**Ye shall not add unto the word** which I command you, **neither shall ye diminish *ought* from it**, that ye may keep the commandments of the LORD your God which I command you" (Deuteronomy 4:2).

God is concerned about exact words. He knew that Satan would try to get man to add to or take away from His words. He said through Solomon: "**Add thou not unto his words**, lest he reprove thee, and thou be found a liar." (Proverbs 30:6).

When God spoke to the prophet Jeremiah, He said: "Thus saith the LORD; Stand in the court of the LORD'S house, and speak unto all the cities of Judah, which come to worship in the LORD'S house, **all the words that I command thee** to speak unto them; **diminish not a word**:" (Jeremiah 26:2).

God could not be any clearer. In order for a Bible to be a true and reliable translation, it must preserve the exact meanings of the original. (For more information about the faulty translation of modern Bibles, see ***Why They Changed the Bible: One World Bible for One World Religion.***)

A Faithfully Passed-Down Bible

There are many of Jesus' sayings in the four Gospels. But some of those sayings were so important that God made sure they were written more than once. The following statement was recorded three times, in Matthew 24:35; Mark 13:31; and Luke 21:33: *"Heaven and earth shall pass away, but **my words shall not pass away.**"*

If Jesus' words shall not pass away, as He promised, then there must be some place where they can be found.

Jesus did not want His truths to be secret, or hidden. He wanted them to be out in the open, for all to see:

"What I tell you in darkness, that speak ye in light: and what ye hear in the ear, that preach ye upon the housetops" (Matthew 10:27).

If God wanted His words in the open, then we should find them among faithful believers, in plain sight.

So where are they? For King James Bible believers, they have been in the open and used for centuries.

But modern Bible users hold a book that has many changes from our King James Bible, based upon two questionable texts found in remote places:

Codex Sinaiticus, which was unknown until 1844, "found" in an Orthodox monastery in the desert.

Codex Vaticanus, which no one knew of, that suddenly appeared in the Vatican Library in 1475.

Neither of them was allowed near the public eye until the 1860s!

Both of these Bibles omit very important words, phrases and verses, change doctrines, and in the case of Sinaiticus, even teach that Jesus was a man who became the Son of God at his baptism (Read Sinaiticus at Mark 1:1-11)!

And yet both of these books are the faulty foundation for almost all modern Bibles and almost all footnotes differing from the King James Bible.

The King James Bible Provides a Checklist

Deborah and I have always wanted to fly in planes. And now we are finally getting the opportunity. She doesn't like airports. She doesn't like crowds. But boy, does she love the window seat! She loves to watch as we taxi and take off. It's amazing how she can figure out where we are, pretty much day or night, just by looking out the window. She has studied maps, she knows landmarks, and all the years of reading books and looking at pictures have paid off, big time.

They say it's not such a big thing anymore to get a plane in the air. At least, it's nothing compared to the other end: landing the plane. You can do all sorts of mid-course corrections on the way. But landing can only be done one way. You have to know the direction and speed of the wind. You have to know about the weather, and of course, the other planes in your area. There is only one runway that your plane can land on, at any given time. Your plane must land just right.

So, do any of you want a hit-or-miss pilot? What if he suddenly decided he didn't need to talk to air traffic control? What if he thought he could land on a different runway, in a different direction? He wouldn't be a pilot for long – and we might not survive the trip. At least, it wouldn't be pleasant.

In short, we want a very narrow-minded pilot. We want someone who does every little thing "by the book."

Deborah and I got a rare privilege. A brother in Christ, who is a pilot, let us go through his checklist. It was two pages long. And every item had to be checked off. If it didn't work right, there was no flight. There were no shortcuts. There is only one way to prepare that plane for flight: the right way.

So how come people are so sloppy about the very words of God? The Creator and Sustainer of the universe has lowered Himself to give us His rules and regulations, His principles and promises, His blessings and cursings. They are all there in one holy Book. So why do we treat it as less important than the pilot does his checklist?

In Bible college, one professor had the word BIBLE on her door. It was an acrostic: Basic Instructions Before Leaving Earth.

If the Ruler of the universe has given you the secret to happiness and joy and fulfillment in this life, and rewards and blessings in the next, wouldn't you want to grab that Book and learn it, and live it, and be blessed?

I would. And I do.

And you can, too.

Just be sure to have the RIGHT checklist.

You've got to know what God wants.

So many people have lives full of adversity. I have so many Facebook friends who are going through difficult times. In fact, there are so many that I'm convinced it's pretty much everybody that experiences hard times, at some point or points in their lives.

Well, guess what? We need to be able to navigate through those tough times. We need a Bible. And we need to get the right Bible, because we want the information that will give us the best results. And the only information like that comes straight from the heart of God Himself. When you have (and follow) God's own advice for your life, you are guaranteed to have the best results, that please God and help you!

In short: **You need to decide on your guide.** There is going to be a judgment. And just because we are Christians does not mean we are not going to be judged.

1 Peter 4:17 For the time *is come* that judgment must begin at the house of God: and if *it* first *begin* at us, what shall the end *be* of them that obey not the gospel of God?

Proverbs 11:31 Behold, the righteous shall be recompensed in the earth: much more the wicked and the sinner.

God *wants* to reward us. Here's what He told Paul:

1 Corinthians 3:11-15 For other foundation can no man lay than that is laid, which is Jesus Christ. Now if any man build upon this foundation gold, silver, precious stones, wood, hay, stubble; Every man's work shall be made manifest: for the day shall declare it, because it shall be revealed by fire; and the fire shall try every man's work of what sort it is. ***If any man's work abide which he hath built thereupon, he shall receive a reward.*** If any man's work shall be burned, he shall suffer loss: but he himself shall be saved; yet so as by fire.

And He said through the apostle John:

2 John 8 *Look to yourselves*, that we lose not those things which we have wrought, but *that we receive a full reward.*

Now there are a lot of people who want to be your guide, to prepare you for that judgment. But you have something better: The Judge Himself has offered to be your Guide. Which will you choose?

It's a no-brainer, right? But believe it or not, the vast majority of Christians have decided, at least for now, that they will trust someone or something *else* to prepare them.

Here's the thing. At this judgment:

There are no deals

There are no appeals

There are no plea bargains
All decisions are final

Did you note that part of 1 Corinthians 3:15? "…he shall suffer loss…"

God has so many things prepared for us who love Him. Think of this: He has a storehouse of wisdom that He is willing to open to us *in this life*, if we read and pray and meditate on His scriptures. Take a look:

Proverbs 2:6-7 For the LORD giveth wisdom: out of his mouth *cometh* knowledge and understanding. ***He layeth up sound wisdom for the righteous***: *he is* a buckler to them that walk uprightly.

I don't know about you, but I *want* that wisdom! And I *want* those rewards! And I have spent years begging God for the opportunity to serve Him. I'd be lower than groundwater if I didn't push as hard as I can to reach for that wisdom and read and trust His holy words!

And besides, His words are what are going to judge us in the last day.

Jesus said, "He that rejecteth me, and receiveth not my words, hath one that judgeth him: *the word that I have spoken, the same shall judge him in the last day*" (John 12:48).

And Jesus is judging Christians, just as surely as He will judge the unsaved.

So, as you prepare for that Day, ask yourself: do you really want to take a chance that maybe fallible human beings found something that God missed? Or do you want the Bible that He bore solid witness to, for over 400 years?

I want to be ready. And God did His part: He placed His holy words in our frail human hands. Let's go for it! What do we have to lose? We definitely have everything to gain.

My first pastor, Dr. Kenneth R.T. Gordon of Montclair First Baptist Church, had a membership class I attended back in late 1980.

One day he wanted to teach us about grace.

He held a small box in his hand. It was wrapped up like a present. Pastor Gordon said, "Grace is like this present. It's a gift. Now, if any of you wants this gift, just come and take it out of my ha—"

I snatched that thing before he finished his sentence.

I got a free tie-tack I stuck in my tie for years. I have no idea what a woman would have done with it. But see, it was a *gift*. And I had just come out of the occult to repent and return to the God who saved my soul eight years before.

I wasn't playing games now. If God had something for me, I wanted it.

That's what God wants us to do, right now, with His words. Will you trust anyone less with your eternal rewards, and true joy and fulfillment in this life?

God bless you as you take that next step.

PART 3 – THE SUPERIORITY OF THE KING JAMES BIBLE

Daniel 12:4: "Many shall run to and fro, and knowledge shall be increased."

In this section I'll show you the history that your teachers never told you. They didn't know it. I didn't even know it, until last year. And yet it's all there. Information that people said didn't exist —I found.

Why?

Because many went to and fro, and knowledge was increased (Daniel 12:4). The more we have learned, the more reasons we have today to talk about the superiority of the King James Bible. But you know what? If you have God's words, you don't have to worry anymore about where they are or whether you can find them.

You don't even have to "go to and fro." You know exactly what God said, right where you are. All that remains is to obey it.

New information can clarify, or even contradict, what we have assumed about history. For instance, new information has shown the story about Codex Sinaiticus to be bogus. It was sold to the world as the "oldest and best" ancient Bible. I used modern research tools and available resources to prove that it is likely a fake. (See ***Is the "World's Oldest Bible" a Fake?***)

While the world is frantically going to and fro, I want to show you how you can plant your faith solidly on the words God preserved in His Book. You can declare: "Thus saith the

Lord!" You don't need to run to and fro in doubt, like everybody else.

Remember, there are people who HATE the King James Bible. When I came to Bible college, I was told: 90-something percent of all Bibles are the same. But don't you DARE trust that King James Bible! That's a BAD BOOK!

Has anyone you know heard that in Bible college? I want you to think about this. They will tell you, and they did from the first day of my Bible college, that all Bibles are the same, *except the King James.* That doesn't even make sense, does it?

What Has The King James Bible Done For The World?

It has shaped Godly believers. Can anybody doubt that? The people of faith came from the King James Bible. During more than 400 years we have seen a clear pattern in churches that believe and use the King James Bible. It has instructed generations of disciples. Their moral compasses were set toward Christ by the King James scriptures.

This pattern takes the form of a life cycle, often expressed as: "the man, the movement, the monument." At first the people repent and turn to God with a deep commitment, after their sin is exposed to God's standards in the Bible. The next generation is often the children of the first group, as well as people they won to Christ. By now it is a movement. These people historically have not had the deep commitment that was there in the beginning. The move switches from godliness (obeying God out of love for Him) to morality (doing right, just because it's right). Christian fervor lags in proportion to their commitment to God's word. Sadly, many stop reading or trusting the King James Bible, and many drift away. But God always has a remnant. Those few seek God anew, and the cycle begins again. Often, this new group separates from the old and forms a new group or denomination.

As you saw in this cycle, godliness and love for the King James Bible go hand-in-hand. Denominations who are straying from the KJV devolve into dealing with schisms over such moral issues as divorce, same-sex marriage, abortion and general worldliness.

It turned the wicked from their ways. As you saw above, that's because when they came to the KJV, they could find out what they'd done that was wicked. Then they could deal with their sins before God.

Without one Bible, people lack a standard for godliness. Other translations allow "wiggle room" that worldly people gladly exploit to allow their particular sins. The King James allows for none of that. For instance, where various "progressive" translations use terms for homosexuality or prostitution in 1 Corinthians 6:9, the King James shows that God's standard is even higher: He doesn't even want men to be "effeminate." That wipes out a whole massive category of offenses and goes way beyond what most modern Bibles are comfortable with. God's standard for godliness is clear in the King James. And the wicked know it. Modern translations only muddy the water with worldly alternative lifestyles.

It leaves no room for self-righteousness. You cannot go to the KJV and justify your sin. Just try! I know, because I get convicted, just about every single day, when I read my Bible. There's something in there that convicts me. It doesn't let us "have it our own way." It's not a "Burger King Bible." You cannot pick and choose. It's not the MCV —the Multiple

Choice Version— that allows you to choose your own doctrine. Nope. The King James isn't like that.

IT'S THE FINAL AUTHORITY. It has the final say, even over our own opinions. So we can have any opinion we want. I have friends on Facebook. I have had friends for decades who have all sorts of differing theological, eschatological, soteriological *opinions*. But the KJV is the *Final Authority*.

We can argue about how well we understand what it says. We can argue about the words. I'm not even going to go to the Hebrew or the Greek to argue about it. I'm going to go by the English words, and *only* these words. If it has stated, we do not get to speculate. This seems like Bible 101, doesn't it?

But if you go into Bible college or seminary, you have to know where your faith is before you go. They are good at persuading people out of trusting the King James. *Know your facts.*

IT GIVES CLEAR DOCTRINES. You can read two parallel verses in modern Bibles and end up with two different doctrines. Three words can make a lot of difference. In Ephesians 1:7 in modern Bibles, it says this: "In him we have redemption through his blood, the forgiveness of sins..."(NIV) But in the parallel, in Colossians 1:14, three words are missing: "in whom we have redemption, the forgiveness of sins."(NIV) The words "through his blood" are missing. Jesus didn't just pay a price to forgive our sins. Something had to be the payment. What was it? There's something missing. Hebrews 9:22 tells us: "...and without shedding of blood is no remission."

It's the blood of the sinless Lamb of God that got us our forgiveness! That's what God was teaching the Hebrews through all those Old Testament sacrifices. But the blood is missing from Colossians in modern Bibles. Preachers have gone so far as to say the blood of Christ is not important. Removing these words helps boost their lie. We are redeemed "...with the precious blood of Christ, as of a lamb without blemish and without spot" (1 Peter 1:19).

Taking out those three words muddies the doctrine of the blood of Christ paying for our sins. I'm not saying it may happen or *will* happen. I'm just pointing out what ***already happened***.

You can go into 1 John 5:7-8 in modern versions and find where they have removed the clearest words defining the Godhead in the Bible.

My own Greek professor in Bible college trusted the twistable rules of textual criticism over the inspiration of God. You see, if you remove those words about the Godhead, the resulting Greek text makes no grammatical sense. Only with those crucial words does the passage make sense. But my professor would rather believe that John wrote his Greek incorrectly, than admit that the words about the Godhead belong in 1 John 5:7. But since John wrote by inspiration of God, then he is really saying that ***God*** made that mistake. I don't believe in that kind of God.

They tell us, "What it says in your King James Bible isn't right." But the reading their textual criticism claims is right, doesn't even make Greek sense.

Let me state this clearly: ***God makes sense.*** His words make sense. And the King James gives us those clear, sensible doctrines.

IT LIFTS UP THE LORD JESUS CHRIST. If you read the King James Bible, you will never have a problem knowing who the Lord Jesus Christ is. But if you were a Gnostic, that's a different thing altogether. On my dad's side, I was largely raised in the Church of Religious Science.

PART 3 – THE SUPERIORITY OF THE KING JAMES BIBLE

Religious Science, Christian Science, Unity, Divine Science, groups related to Phinehas P. Quimby and the New Thought Movement, —all of those movements that started in the 1800s— are basically occultism. They separate out Jesus from "the Christ."

"The Christ" was this being or "self" or other identity that can come upon an occultic practitioner, possibly in his or her final reincarnation. (I found that out when I read the "deeper" occult books in Unity.) According to the teaching, at that point he or she is supposed to take on various powers, until they are received as Christ or maybe killed like Jesus and go on to their "next existence" —to Nirvana, or Philadelphia, or wherever.

The whole idea behind the removal of "Lord," "Jesus," or "Christ" from various scriptures was that the ancient Gnostics (and their modern counterparts) separated the Lord -- God, Jesus -- the man, and Christ -- the Messiah. It ruined their doctrine if He were considered all three at the same time. (Too bad —He was and still is!)

When we look in these other Bibles, we find that they separated these three characteristics of the Lord Jesus Christ. Gnostics had to do it, because they didn't believe they were joined as the same Person. They separated them. But the King James lifts up the Lord as Jesus and Christ, without apology.

IT DOESN'T JUSTIFY SINS. You just can't get away with *anything* with this Book. Check out my testimony. I've got a lot of stuff out on youtube.com/c/chicktracts. Or go to www.chick.com/Bible. You can click on YouTube from there. If you look at my testimony, you'll find out that the Lord taught me about my sins. He, Himself, taught me, after I'd conjured up a storm as a 17-year-old who was deep in the occult —after

I'd received the Lord 8 years earlier. Sometimes that happens, when you have no instruction in the Lord.

But when God brought me back 8 years later, it was with the King James Bible. And that left me no "wiggle room." I was guilty —and I knew it.

IT DOESN'T REQUIRE KNOWLEDGE OF GREEK AND HEBREW. I've heard testimonies like this: "I never learned Greek, I never learned Hebrew. I never learned any foreign languages. I never learned any deep theology. But I did memorize this Book." Well, there you go. You can have an incredible life that pleases God… without a lick of Greek.

But once you enter Bible college, they want you to learn everything else *but* Bible. They'll tell you about "the Greek" and "the Hebrew." But that's not all.

IT DOESN'T REQUIRE READING COMMENTARIES. Professors will also tell you that you have to consult "the commentaries" to understand the *true* meaning of the Bible. I had entire classes whose homework consisted of consulting the commentaries and making my own commentary on every verse using other commentaries. I'm not kidding.

Well, guess what? After I realized I could trust the King James, I did a study with commentaries. It was amazing. I found out that one commentator quotes some guy from before him. And then the commentator after him quotes the two. And this guy after him quotes the three. And this guy after him quotes the four. And this guy after him quotes the five. Get the picture?

Then each later commentator picks and chooses which previous comments **he** likes, and which ideas **he** doesn't like. And then *in **his** commentary* suddenly he acts all authoritative about *his* view, because **he** quoted a certain guy at a certain point on a certain doctrine that agreed with *him!* The authorities he quoted then made it appear that *his* opinion **must** be right. That's what the Pharisees did!

I tried something out. You are welcome to do it, too, if you want. It's a fun exercise. I was always able to find at least one of these commentators who agreed with the King James Bible at any particular verse. Just like they were able to find a commentator who disagreed with any given verse of the King James Bible. It's all pointless! Why not just believe the King James Bible?

They pick and choose, in order to make yet another commentary. But I trust this Book, the King James Bible. That means I can spend more time obeying God's words, than questioning them.

IT IS "AN EQUAL OPPORTUNITY OFFENDER." If you have a doctrinal system, the KJV will offend you, because it will not fit your doctrinal system, no matter what you do. You can try and try, but you will get to some verses that will just upset you. Something about the words will not fit the vocabulary of your doctrinal system. I can almost guarantee it.

I read one book that will remain unmentioned, where the author, seemingly a King James believer, sided with an Alexandrian text, because it fit his scenario for the Day of the Lord! If you have to change the Bible to fit your doctrine -- you're not doing it right.

You will want to reinterpret those verses when they do not make you feel good. That's because God does not fit in man's box. God never said He did. And neither do His words fit in man's box in the King James Bible.

It doesn't contradict itself. The most basic principle of textual criticism, from Johann Albrecht Bengel, is "The harder reading is to be preferred." In other words, *the less-clear words are more likely original than the ones that make perfect sense.*

Let me put this another way. We were taught that ancient copyists edited the Bibles as they copied them, to make their copy of the Bible smoother and easier to understand. So if they came upon a verse that was less clear to them, they would try to "clean it up" and make it sound like other verses.

Text scholars have a "family tree" of Bibles. They teach that no copyist would take a clear verse and make it unclear. So if there are 2 or more versions of a verse, the one that is the most rough and un-polished would be closer to the original.

But wait. The Bible verse you end up with will always be less clear, contradictory, incorrect in grammar, or have historical or doctrinal problems. So what they end up with in textual criticism is a text that *doesn't make sense!*

And then after those mental gymnastics, these scholars only consider it a "better reading," but they can never settle on what is "the best."

But I believe in a God that **doesn't** make contradictions; I believe in a God that **does** make sense; I believe in the God who **knows** what He's talking about, and He knows how to speak the language. That's all because inspiration "is given of God," not "man's device."

That's why they have to destroy that belief in the Bible, by changing those verses. When you read the new Bibles, you see that those changes and contradictions are there in order to allow the doubting scholars their opinions ⸺and their favorite sins. But that's another topic.

IT BRINGS FAITH. This is the key. One of my first YouTube videos was called: "Some Bibles create FAITH —others DOUBT." I talked about how reading the King James brings faith; but reading the other versions bring doubt. It was my most popular video because people want to have FAITH. And believing and reading the King James brings FAITH.

By contrast, I have found in the last 39 years of my Christian faith, that every other Bible, even a King James lookalike (like the New King James), brings DOUBT.

IT BROUGHT ME CONVICTION AND BOLDNESS.

I had given the New King James 10 years of my life, before I came to trust the King James. It *never* brought me conviction. But within *2 days* of my conviction on reading the King James, I was trying to win the souls of a Jehovah's Witness and his son. Evidently I was so bold about it that it threatened all the Jehovah's Witnesses in my neighborhood!

It was quite a sight. All the women and the children left the street. I have no idea where they went. Then all the men got into formation, 3 by 3, in 7 rows, and started doing a Jericho march around my property! I was on the phone with my friend, Ron, to tell him about how I was just talking to these Jehovah's Witnesses, and I'm looking out my window, and they're marching around, tromping down the street!

So I ran over and said, "HEY! Do any of you understand **Greek?** And one guy comes out. I said, "Come over here! I want you to read this manuscript with me. I want to show you something."

He turned around, and he walked back, found his exact slot, got in it and they continued marching slowly down the street.

I jumped over my fence and called out after them, "I just don't want you to go to **helllll**!!!"

TWO DAYS! Just **two days** trusting and reading a King James Bible. You can't tell me that's just a coincidence. I was *there*. It was *conviction*, not coincidence.

I already had my college and seminary degrees. I had 30-something different Bibles to choose from. I had electronic and physical resources for Bible study. I had more than most. And yet in just TWO DAYS after being convinced that the King James was what God said, translated into English, I was this bold. It's because God produces that kind of conviction when it's His words, without a mixture of man's words!

That's because the *only* words that are inspired are the words that are given by inspiration of GOD!

It Brought Me Doctrinal Clarity.

Which text you choose for your Bible makes a big difference in what you believe.

One of my friends on Facebook had been taught by the writings of a number of Dallas Theological Seminary professors. And she had used the NIV for 20 years before she came to the King James.

We had a conversation one night and I started showing her all the scriptures where Jesus is God on earth. As I started giving them to her, I said, "Do me a favor. Could you get out your NIV?"

She looked up all those verses I had just shown her. She was shocked! Every verse I used to show that Jesus was God on earth was changed in her 1984 NIV. Here are a few of them:

John 3:13

King James:

"And no man hath ascended up to heaven, but he that came down from heaven, even the Son of man **which is in heaven.**"

NIV:

"No one has ever gone into heaven except the one who came from heaven—the Son of Man _____ __ __ _____." (The words are missing.)

. . . .

Philippians 2:7

King James:

"But **made himself of no reputation**, and took upon him the form of a servant, and was made in the likeness of men:"

NIV:

"rather, **he made himself nothing** by taking the very nature of a servant, being made in human likeness."

. . . .

1 Timothy 3:16

King James:

"And without controversy great is the mystery of godliness: **God was manifest in the flesh...**"

NIV:

"Beyond all question, the mystery of godliness is great: **He appeared in a body...**"

. . . .

John 9:35

King James:
> "Jesus heard that they had cast him out; and when he had found him, he said unto him, Dost thou **believe on the Son of God?**"

NIV:
> "Jesus heard that they had thrown him out, and when he found him, he said, 'Do you **believe in the Son of Man?**'"

. . . .

Every single one of those verses was changed in the NIV. Every single one! None of those verses said or implied that Jesus was God on earth. Quite a change, huh?

If I only read the NIV in those verses, I'd never know that Jesus was both God and man while He ministered on earth. So church doctrinal statements would be all that was left to claim that Jesus was 100% God and 100% man. The Bible wouldn't even show it anymore. How then could I preach and teach that doctrine with conviction? I couldn't. And that's the place many people are, who don't have the correct words in their Bibles.

The King James, with its powerful words and clear doctrines, changed me from pew-sitter to soul-winner in two days. That's because God produces that kind of conviction when it's His words, without a mixture of man's words!

So you may grow up, raised using the King James. But as you get older, the youth minister or someone who cares about the youth starts saying, "Yeah, but the NIV is easier." That's not really true. It seems like it is, though. But at what cost?

It's like in the book or movie, Pilgrim's Progress. There's one point where there's a pathway right next to the main road. The

PART 3 – THE SUPERIORITY OF THE KING JAMES BIBLE

road was a little rough. That pathway looked a little easier. So switch paths and pretty soon you're waaaaaay off course.

That was the New King James for me. It seemed so close to the King James, but easier. Of course I believed that my Bible college professors knew better. They even knew one of the NKJV translators. One day at lunch a teacher told me, "They say it's just a modified King James. But we know better. It's actually a pretty good translation." What he really meant was that it's a lot like the other non-King James Bibles on the market.

If a non-King James person calls a King James lookalike Bible a "pretty good translation" -- watch out! There's something wrong with it.

Years later I talked about this issue with some Bible college students at another college. The next week they came to me and said, "The professor told us we could only use the NAS, NIV or NRSV. One person asked about the New King James, and he said, 'Okay, the New King James is permitted. But not the King James.'"

That stunned me. If they are really so close, then why permit the one and *forbid* the other? If a modern King James lookalike is permitted by a modern version teacher, you can know that somewhere they crossed a line they shouldn't have.

IT EXPOSED THE COUNTERFEITS. If you want to counterfeit money, do you write "This is a counterfeit" on it? Of course not! You make it look so close to the original that there's only slight little differences that would ever tell you that it's not the real thing.

Don't let anybody fool you, this King James Bible brings FAITH to its readers and its listeners. Romans 10:17: "So then faith cometh by hearing, and hearing by the word of God." Read that again slowly, because it's telling you something.

Romans 10:17: "So then **faith cometh** by hearing, and hearing **by the word of God**."

If FAITH is not the product of reading a Bible version, then maybe it's not the word of God.

Here's something you ought to think about. Scholars started switching the Bible texts in earnest about 1876. Westcott and Hort had already been working on the Greek text and passed it on, bit by bit, to their Revision Committee members. They were sworn to secrecy not to reveal the Greek text. That Greek New Testament came out *one week* before the English Revised Version, in August of 1881.

The American wing of the Committee kept meeting until 1901, when the American Standard Version (then called the American Revised Version) came out.

Now think about it. From that time, either 1881 or 1901, where were the revivals? Which way went the social change? Where was the outpouring of faith that should have followed "rediscovering the actual words of God"?

Tischendorf originally thought he was going to bring about a big revival, that he was going to bring faith to the people to counter "the attacks of doubting science," and prove "the sacred and indestructible foundation of our faith."

When did that revival happen? It didn't. Tischendorf didn't even believe his own words. He was all cow-towing to the pope. He was too busy trying to get ahold of Codex Vaticanus and be the first to fully analyze and publish its text. He would have said or done *anything* (and did, I found out) to get his hands on the pope's book.

PART 3 – THE SUPERIORITY OF THE KING JAMES BIBLE

It Produces Fruit.

Let's talk again about the fruit of the King James Bible. 2011 was the 400th anniversary of the publishing of the King James Bible. A lot of people wrote articles about it. Look at this article by reporter Kathy Lynn Grossman in USA Today. This is a non-King James Bible person. But this is what she wrote on April 21st, 2011.

Bible readers prefer King James version

By Cathy Lynn Grossman, USA TODAY   Updated 4/21/2011 2:54 PM

If thou hast a Bible in the house right now and readeth it at least once a month, chances are strong it's the majestic King James Version of the Bible in Elizabethan English, a new survey out today finds.

By Rhyne Piggott, USA TODAY
The first King James Bible was printed in New York in 1792. The King James version is the Bible most adults own, according to a new survey.

Of the 89% of U.S. adults who own at least one Bible, 67% own a King James, which marks its 400th anniversary this year, according to LifeWay Research, a Nashville-based Christian research agency.

Although there are two dozen English-language Bibles in many contemporary translations, the King James Version reigns even more supreme among those who actually read their Bibles: 82% of those who read the Good Book at least once a month rely on the translation that first brought the Scripture to the English-speaking masses worldwide.

Age makes a difference. Seventy-six percent of Bible owners 55 and older have a King James, compared with 56% of those under 35, according to the survey of 1,004 adults, conducted March 2-6.

"Of the 89% of U.S. adults who own at least one Bible, 67% own a King James..." Did you know that? You'd never know that by the way most scholars talk about it.

Serious Christians prefer it. Have you seen that meme on the internet that says "When you pick up the Bible, the devil gets a headache. When you open it, he collapses"?

What? He doesn't give a flying fig what you do with it.

You can do anything you want with it. You can play golf with it. You can fly it in the air. You can wave it around. You can stand and say, "I believe this Bible. I believe it's the word of God," with a big smile on your face. But it will do you no good if you don't actually believe it, don't read it, don't get convicted by it, and don't do anything with it other than holding it in your hand at the beginning of the church service.

Grossman goes on: "...among those who actually read their Bibles: 82% of those who read the Good Book at least once a month rely on" [the King James Bible].

Take a look at the chart below. According to a later study, "The Bible in American Life" by Purdue University, between 2011-2016, 55% of Bible readers read the King James. The NIV, so put forward by the media, only had 19% of that readership.

BIBLE TRANSLATIONS USED BY READERS

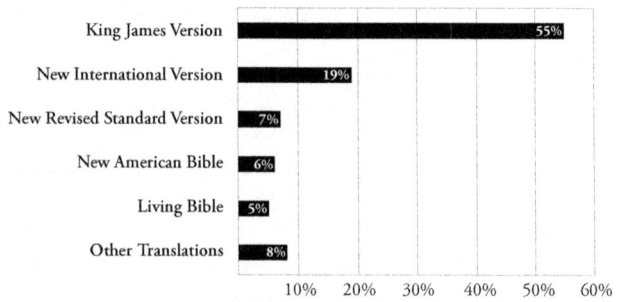

PART 3 – THE SUPERIORITY OF THE KING JAMES BIBLE

Most people didn't know about these statistics. Companies that were putting this information out, though, like LifeWay and the Barna Group, do not believe that the King James Bible is God's preserved words. LifeWay was into selling all the other different versions, and now sadly they are closing their bookstores.

But you've got 55% who actually USE and READ the King James Bible. It's not what we've been told. Let's go on.

There's another item, posted to christianitytoday.com on March 13, 2014.

"The Most Popular and Fastest-Growing Bible Translation Isn't What You Think It Is." But there's more to it. It says, "The translations that most Americans are" (there it is again) "READING" turns out to be the King James Bible.

So, to all of those people who say, "Why are you reading the King James Bible?" You can say, "Do you read YOURS? Tell me about it."

It doesn't matter if you buy every new Anniversary Version of every other Bible there is in the world. If you don't read it, it doesn't do anything. And if you do read it, watch out. There are a lot of pitfalls of doubt built into those Bibles.

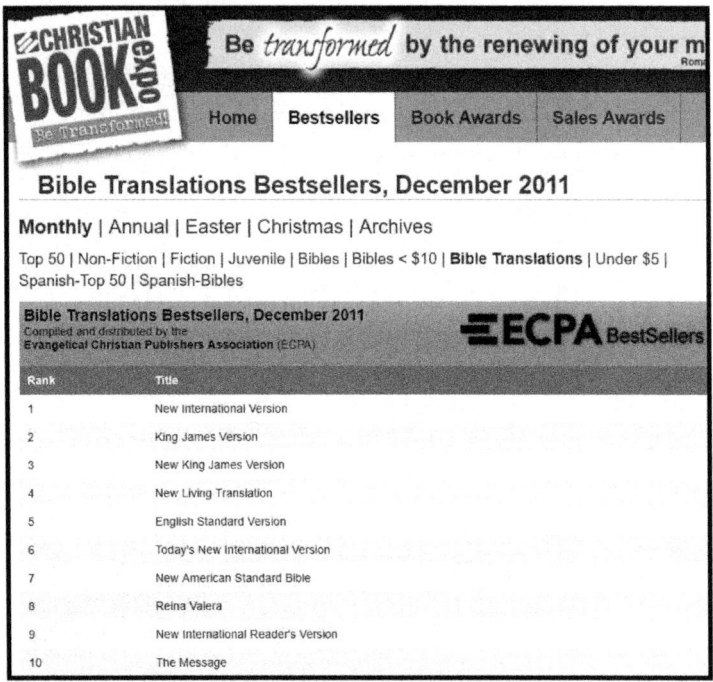

The screen grab above is from the Christian Book Expo. When looking at the sales of Bibles for Christmases from 2011 through 2016-2017, they said that the NIV sold more.

But the King James stayed at #2. It was still #2 in December 2012 and 2013. The New King James had some special promotions and jumped onto the list for Christmas sales.

So they get their Christmas editions. They release the "whatever-the-new-movie-is Bible," the "whatever-the-new-fad-is

Bible." For Christmas 2015 the NKJV was #1. In 2016 the New Living Translation moved up, because of their good selling techniques at Christmas time.

By these techniques, the King James was #3 for Christmas of 2014, 15 and 16. But in Christmas of 2017 and 2018 the King James was back at #2. I decided to keep checking from December of 2018, month by month, right through April. The NIV stayed at #1 and the KJV at #2. So that is the trend, according to Christian Book Expo (christianbookexpo.com).

These statistics are *only* from certain mainline publishers, ignoring scores of publishers of King James Bibles that are spread around the world, even in the millions. One single shipment sent to Papua New Guinea by BIMI (Baptist International Missions, Inc.) contained 165,000 King James Bibles! Their goal is one King James Bible for every man, woman and child in the country (population: over 8 million). And by the way, the King James Bible is now the official Bible of Papua New Guinea (much to the chagrin of the United Bible Societies)!

The statistics I mentioned do not include many other churches and companies that publish King James Bibles. For instance, Bearing Precious Seed, Bible & Literature Missionary Foundation, The Bible for Today (the Defined Bible by DA Waite), Trinitarian Bible Society, Church Bible Publishers, Local Church Bible Publishers --they don't include *any* of these. How many King James Bibles have these companies made, and sold, and people read? I bought Bibles from these guys, and they never made it on that website's list. How many others bought Bibles from them, just like me?

It is not tainted with secular publishers. Who are the publishers on these lists? Zondervan, World, Thomas Nelson, Catholic publishers of various kinds. Now let's look at a few more facts about these publishers: In 1988 HarperCollins acquired Zondervan. So now everything that Zondervan has, and everything HarperCollins has are all on that one list.

In 2003 Thomas Nelson had acquired World Bible Publishers. So those two became one. But then they added another division called Catholic Bible Press. Did you know that Thomas Nelson had a Catholic subdivision?

I had one of their Bibles. I sat there looking at it and did a double-take. It said: "Catholic Bible Press, a division of Thomas Nelson" right there on the copyright page.

In 2012 HarperCollins bought Thomas Nelson. Now it's an even larger company. So a secular parent company, News Corporation, owns: HarperCollins, Zondervan, Thomas Nelson, World, Catholic Bible Press (and other Catholic Bibles), along with other publishers.

Now News Corporation controls 55% of all Bible production. Do you think that might skew the numbers a bit? Do you think they have a vested interest in selling other Bibles, made by their subsidiaries? They do. They'll do anything and everything to sell other Bibles.

But if Christians truly trust the King James Bible as God's holy and preserved words, what do you think the bottom line on all the other Bible versions will be? They'll be on a sale table faster than you can say "Fake News!"

That's also why, when they *do* publish King James study Bibles, most of them are laced with doubting notes, to get you to buy all their other stock of doubt-building Bibles.

PART 3 – THE SUPERIORITY OF THE KING JAMES BIBLE

Faith is caused by ONE BIBLE as God's words, instead of DOUBT caused by a multitude of Bibles. FAITH vs. DOUBT.

IT RESCUED ME FROM THE CONFUSION IN BIBLE COLLEGE AND SEMINARY.

I was well-known in Bible college, because I had multiple versions that I kept in my backpack, along with my Greek New Testament. I would sit in Chapel and sometimes other students would forget their Bibles. I would pass out Bibles to everybody —well, so-called Bibles, no King Jameses!

Then I'd sit there in chapel with the Greek. Soon, when I had questions, I acquired my Rienecker *Linguistic Key to the Greek New Testament*, my Zerwick-Grosvenor *A Grammatical Analysis of the Greek New Testament* (Jesuit, by the way), and soon got other Greek helps and manuscripts that I would check --and stuff into my backpack. I had a very full backpack.

I was never sure of exactly what I believed. And I was a zealot. But I couldn't be sure, because I believed my professors. Please understand: the majority of professors, the majority of preachers, ministers, deacons, lay people who have gone to any kind of college, have been taught this: DOUBT, not FAITH. My professors considered it a weakness and a naïve mind, if you believed what the King James Bible said.

There are 88 Bibles in the current list of regular published Bibles you can find right now: the King James and 87 others. And all of their publishers want to make money off of their versions. If they don't sell them, that's a lot of stock to have to write off. That hurts their bottom line. *They are more interested in selling product than in people believing the truth.*

But among all these English Bibles the King James is the most read English Bible in the world. I want you to realize how **powerful** that is.

People don't know this fact because they've been deceived by the media hype.

Its Words Have Power.

So what should we expect if they are God's words? Jeremiah 23:29: "Is not my word like as a **fire**? saith the LORD; and like a **hammer** that breaketh the rock in pieces?"

That's what God's words do. When you read them, they hit you. They're supposed to, because they're from God. They're holy. We're not; He is!

Isaiah 55:11 "So shall my word be that goeth forth out of my mouth..." (Whose word? God's word.) "...it shall not return unto me void, but it shall accomplish that which I please, and it shall prosper in the thing whereto I sent it." So if somebody is throwing an NIV at somebody, and godly change is not happening, it's because it's not the word of God. It doesn't have the seal of God's approval on it.

I'm not trying to be mean. It's just true. I know of two people with deliverance ministries trying to cast out devils. One trusted the King James Bible, and the other was using an NIV. It's really true. I talked to him.

In fact, the people with the one ministry talked to the guy with the King James in the other ministry, and said, "Can you deal with this guy?" They had done what had worked before, but the devil didn't leave this particular person. So they asked the King James guy to have a whack at it. And the devil was cast out. And at the end they said, (it sounds like a Bible verse), "Why could not we cast him out?" He said, "Because you didn't have the word of God." And the devils know. They can laugh at it. But God's words have **power**. You can't fake that.

Deuteronomy 4:2 "Ye shall not add unto the word which I command you, neither shall ye diminish ought from it, that ye may keep the commandments of the LORD your God which I command you." If you have a Bible that willy-nilly adds to and takes away from God's words, the devils know. They know they don't have to respect those words. Believe those preachers who tell you the Devil is a legalist. He is. He's bound by the words of God. But I guarantee you, he is not bound by the opinions of men, who change God's words to what they wish God said, instead of giving us word for word what God inspired and delivered to man.

Don't mess with a book mixed with man's words. There's no tricking God: He knows what's in His book. And there's no tricking the devils, either. They know the Bible better than you do. And the King James tells us exactly what we need to know, because it is an accurate translation of what God said. It's not an interpretation by men, like modern Bibles.

IT TELLS US WHAT GOD WANTS FROM US. What is the purpose of having God's words? So you know what commandments you're supposed to keep.

Deuteronomy 4:10 "...Gather me the people together, and I will make them hear my words..."

And look at the result: "...that they may learn to fear me..."

Guess what's missing in our culture right now? Not just words in Bible versions, but the fear of the Lord. Instead, it's the "*awe* of the Lord!" or It's the "*great respect for* the Lord."

No. God says it's the *fear* of the Lord. And he wants them to learn to fear Him "...all the days that they shall live upon the earth..."

Then God adds "...and *that* they may teach their children." How many of these people with modern Bibles are teaching their children the word of God? Not a lot. I only say it because I've been around them. And over three decades I've watched their kids grow up without that solid instruction in the word that should have come from their parents. It's sad where a lot of them end up.

In Deuteronomy 18:18 God promised Moses, "I will raise them up a Prophet from among their brethren, like unto thee, and will put my words in his mouth; and he shall speak unto them all that I shall command him." "*All.*" "Most" isn't good enough. God continually tells us that he wants us to read, and to pass on, *all* that He has said.

IT GIVES US THE VERY WORDS OF GOD. When I was a student under David Allan Hubbard, the former head of Fuller Seminary, he was my teacher for Hebrew literature. And he said more than once, "It's the 'word' of God, not the 'words' of God," meaning it's 'the general message.'

That's the same teacher who, when he came to the prophet Ezekiel, said that chapters 40-48 were Ezekiel's "wish fulfillment dream." According to Hubbard, Ezekiel hoped there would be a religious reformation and an enlarged and restored temple. But alas, it didn't happen. To him, it was not the words of the holy God given to Ezekiel. It was merely a product of the prophet's imagination.

So that was the president of Fuller Seminary, my seminary. There's a library dedicated to him now. Reject God's words and teach others, get a library with your name on it. *Nah*, it's not worth it.

Rewards in heaven for trusting and obeying God are worth *way* more than monuments on earth for pleasing man. As

God said in James 3:1, "My brethren, be not many masters, knowing that we shall receive the greater condemnation."

Let's go back to Jesus. In John 14:10 He said, "Believest thou not that I am in the Father, and the Father in me? the **words** that I speak unto you I speak not of myself: but the Father that dwelleth in me, he doeth the works." God had said, I'll "put my **words** in his mouth" in Deuteronomy 18:18. Jesus was that fulfillment to the prophecy.

Again, Jesus said the Father *put* His words in Jesus' mouth. There's this connection here, between Jesus and His Father. Jesus' words *were* His Father's words.

If you want to talk to a Jehovah's Witness, you can use that. God says in Isaiah 59:21, "As for me, this is my covenant with them, saith the LORD; My spirit that is upon thee, and **my words**..." (there they are) "...which I have put in thy mouth, shall not depart out of thy mouth..."

That's a promise. Do you know how you can fulfill that promise in your life? By having the words of God, and getting them into you, by reading them, memorizing them, being convicted by them, seeking God over them, and having God change you through them.

IT IS PERMANENT ENOUGH TO PASS TO NEXT GENERATION. If you have His words in a Book, they won't depart out of your mouth. Then they can be passed to the next generation. God continued in Isaiah 59:21, "...nor out of the mouth of thy seed, nor out of the mouth of thy seed's seed, saith the LORD, from henceforth and for ever."

How many of you want to have godly kids, and grandkids, and great-grandkids, and great-great-grandkids, if the Lord tarry? I do. Jeremiah testified in Jeremiah 1:9 "Then the LORD put forth his hand and touched my mouth. And the LORD said unto me, Behold, **I have put my words** in thy mouth." Look at that. God made Jeremiah His prophet, so He put his exact words into Jeremiah's mouth, just like He would later put them in Jesus' mouth. That's the high calling of a prophet of God.

The Sadducees were a messed-up bunch because they didn't believe in two important things: they didn't believe in a bodily resurrection from the dead and they didn't believe in —the *prophets*. God said He put His words in the mouth of this prophet. There's no escaping it: you have to believe the prophets, because God's words were in them.

2 Chronicles 20:20 "… Jehoshaphat stood and said, Hear me, O Judah, and ye inhabitants of Jerusalem; Believe in the LORD your God, so shall ye be established; **believe his prophets**, so shall ye prosper."

Luke 24:25 "Then he [Jesus] said unto them, O fools, and slow of heart to **believe all that the prophets have spoken:**"

We have to believe the prophets. Jesus Himself said so.

Fenton John Anthony Hort, a father of modern doubting Bibles, wrote that a prophet only leaned on his own understanding of "all that is going on around him… coloured by the events, the thoughts, and the feelings of his own time, which take hold on his own heart…"[1] That's what the Holy Ghost somehow "inspired." And that is exactly what I heard from the president of Fuller.

Except that's not what happened. The prophets were given a message, sometimes for generations after them. And the exact words were so important, that the Holy Ghost had to put it

---

1) See *Village Sermons* (London: MacMillan and Co., 1897), pp. 209-210. Available on www.books.google.com.

inside them. And it burned. Jeremiah had to say it, because he couldn't NOT say it.

Jeremiah 5:14 "Wherefore thus saith the LORD God of hosts, Because ye speak this word, behold, I will make my words in thy mouth fire, and this people wood, and it shall devour them." And Jeremiah's a teenager, commanded to speak to a lot of powerful, rebellious adults! I bet he felt greatly intimidated to change his message to make it more palatable to the multitudes. But here's the thing. The "thoughts and feelings of his own time" didn't matter. What mattered were the words of God.

That's why God commanded Jeremiah in 26:2: "…**all the words** that I command thee to speak unto them; **diminish not a word**:" And that's why we still have those words today. They don't pass away when they're God's. He sees to it, being God and all.

God continued this theme with Jeremiah in 6:19: "Hear, O earth: behold, I will bring evil upon this people, even the fruit of their thoughts, because they have not hearkened unto **my words**, nor to my law, but rejected it."

How could you possibly hearken unto it, if you don't know what "it" is?

Listen to God's indictment of teachers and preachers and parents, all over the world.

Jeremiah 23:22 "But if they had stood in my counsel, and had caused my people to hear **my words**, then they should have turned them from their evil way, and from the evil of their doings."

Think about it. People all over the world are not causing the people to hear God's words. They're hearing something else: a mixture of men's opinions, but not His words.

Its message is respected by atheists. There's a performer, Penn Jillette. He's one of those magicians who tells you his secrets when he does his magic and stuff... And he's a hardened atheist.

My friend, Tim Berends, has been a radio personality for decades. He also passes out about 300 tracts a day in Las Vegas. One day, he gave Penn Jillette' a King James Bible. Penn claimed that he has read the Bible through four times. Penn posted a video on his YouTube vlog. I've transcribed part of it below:

> *"...I don't respect people who don't proselytize... If you believe that there's a heaven and a hell, and people could be going to hell or not getting eternal life, or whatever, and you think that, well, it's not really worth telling them this because it would make it socially awkward — and atheists who think that people shouldn't proselytize, 'Just leave me alone; keep your religion to yourself'— how much do you have to hate somebody to not proselytize? How much do you have to hate somebody to believe that everlasting life is possible and not tell them that? I mean, if I believed, beyond the shadow of a doubt, that a truck was coming at you, and you didn't believe it, that truck was bearing down on you, there is a certain point where I tackle you. And this is more important than that."*

Wow! What an honest guy! That's amazing. That's Penn Jillette of Penn & Teller. If you remember that name, Penn Jillette, pray for him, because I'd love for him to get saved. He's really messed up.

It doesn't "steal" God's words. Look at the following verse in a different way. Think of this as the false Bible versions, and it could change your life.

Jeremiah 23:30-31 "Therefore, behold, I am against the prophets, saith the LORD, that steal **my words** every one from his neighbour. Behold, I am against the prophets, saith the LORD, that use their tongues, and say, He saith."

False Bible versions change God's holy words, and then claim to be a "Bible." Think of the Message Bible or the Living Bible. They claim to be a Bible, God's words. And yet they add and take away words almost at random! They steal God's words and claim "He saith!" just like God said in the passage above.

Back when I went to PCC, Pacific Christian College, the church nearest us had replaced the pew Bibles with NIVs. The older members looked at the cover, and said, "They can't say that!" The cover of the NIV said, "Holy Bible." They said, "It's a Bible; but it's not the Holy Bible." Even they, not using the King James, knew that the NIV didn't deserve the name "Holy Bible." That tells you something.

If your Bible steals God's words, and stuffs them into a footnote or eliminates them altogether (see my book, *Look What's Missing,* for a list of words stolen from 257 verses), then just like with those prophets, God is against that Bible version.

IT IS RESPECTED ABOVE THE MODERN VERSIONS. Those people I told you about just now? They most likely grew up reading the King James Bible. And even with no evidence like what I've been putting in books for over 15 years, *they knew the difference.* They respected the King James. They didn't respect the NIV.

Remember? Even today, 55% of people who actually read the Bible, prefer to read the King James Bible. It's that respected. Two verses before, God had said to Jeremiah:

"The prophet that hath a dream, let him tell a dream; and he that hath **my word**, let him speak **my word** faithfully. What is the chaff to the wheat? saith the LORD" (Jeremiah 23:28).

People have sent me mail and email, containing the same story numerous times over the years: they've sat in church and the pastor has gotten out some "chaff" Bible to read. And "It just didn't *feel* right," or "It felt *wrong*." Even if they didn't know why, they knew that much. And many of them weren't even King James people —yet! There's just no comparison.

IT DOESN'T MIX IN THE OCCULT. They "use their tongues, and say, He saith."(Jer. 23:31) One example of putting words in God's mouth is the Message Bible. I say it's half-right. It *is* a mess. And if you throw a "new" in the middle, it's a "Mess (New) Age Bible." Because either the guy was an occultist, or he just liked replacing God's words with occultic terminology.[2]

That's why in the Lord's Prayer, the Message Bible doesn't say "in earth as it is in heaven." It says, "As above, so below." That's the Baphomet. That's the basic principle taught by Hermes Trismegistus, the first occultic teaching I ever read, and its right there in that "Bible." Incidentally, Eugene Peterson, the author passed away in October of 2018. He knows better now.

IT TELLS US WHO THE FALSE PROPHETS ARE. Why did they "*use their tongues*, and say, He saith"? Jeremiah 29:19 says "Because they have not hearkened to **my words**, saith the LORD, which I sent unto them by my servants the prophets, rising up early and sending them; but ye would not hear, saith the LORD."

God sent those prophets. God sent His word. Just like He

---

2) See Warren Smith, *Deceived on Purpose: the New Age Implications of the Purpose-Driven Church* (Mountain Stream Press, 2nd ed. 2004), pp. 29-35.

PART 3 – THE SUPERIORITY OF THE KING JAMES BIBLE

gave them His words every day, we've had His words since 1611, since the rise of the printing press.

Look at Ezekiel 2:7 "And thou shalt speak **my words** unto them, whether they will hear, or whether they will forbear: for they are most rebellious." And see Ezekiel 2:4-5 "For they are impudent children and stiffhearted. I do send thee unto them; and thou shalt say unto them, Thus saith the Lord GOD."

They "used *their* tongues," only because they changed God's words. Translating God's words accurately, by formal equivalence, is not "using their tongues." They are using God's. But when they decide that their own thoughts are more important to convey than God's words, that's the point at which they "use their tongues," instead of saying exactly what God gave us, and become false prophets.

IT CARRIES THE SAME WEIGHT AS THE PROPHETS. It's not good enough to say, "Thus saith the NIV!" or "Thus saith the ESV!" Not at all! We must be able to say: "Thus saith the Lord God." When I hold up a King James Bible, I really believe I can say that. I've said this repeatedly online, *"I may not understand every word of this Book, but I believe every word of this Book."*

There is an easy way to tell which type of scholar made a Bible. The scholars of **faith** believed God's words and *transmitted* them to us in our language. The scholars of **doubt**, who disbelieved God's words, substituted their own words and then claimed, "He saith."

God's words, translated accurately, are just as weighty as the words originally pronounced or read by the prophets God sent.

I did a teaching about Ahaziah. I figured out how King Ahaziah appears to be 22 and 42 at the same time, in 2 Kings and 2 Chronicles. You can see it on the YouTube channel for yourself. My solution doesn't contradict a single verse of the Bible. It took me four years just to figure out how to work the numbers. I could do this *only* because I had a literal transmission of God's exact words in my language. Every commentary I used only led me to disaster and despair.

Let's continue with Ezekiel 2:5 "And they, whether they will hear, or whether they will forbear… yet shall know that there hath been a prophet among them." When you speak the words of the KJV, you're just like a prophet, because you're speaking THE WORDS of God.

It promises good to the upright. Micah 2:7 "O thou that art named the house of Jacob, is the spirit of the LORD straitened? are these his doings? **do not my words do good to him that walketh uprightly?**"

Read that again. That's a promise. That's better than any kind of faith-healing promise you can come up with.

It says if you walk uprightly, God's words will do good to you. That's pretty awesome!

It pronounces shame on those ashamed of His words. Consider Zechariah 1:6: "But **my words** and my statutes, which I commanded my servants the prophets, did they not take hold of your fathers? …"

What did God say His words would do? God's words and statutes were meant to *take hold of* those who read them. That's *very personal* between God and us. And it's a promise we can grab hold of now, any time we read His holy words. In seminary, they called this the "I-Thou" relationship, where God is standing in front of us and talks to us directly. We can have that, prayerfully reading the King James Bible!

"Whosoever therefore shall be ashamed of me and of my words in this adulterous and sinful generation; of him also shall the Son

of man be ashamed, when he cometh in the glory of his Father with the holy angels" (Mark 8:38).

Here's the picture. We who are saved will eventually stand before Jesus. He'll sit on His throne. He'll have all His Father's glory, nothing held back. The holy angels will also be gathered around. That could be a glorious or a terrifying sight. Talk about intimidated! We will not be happy about *anything* we did that didn't glorify the One who created and will judge the universe, once we realize Who it is we were treating so lightly in this life.

And we who are saved will be rewarded (1 Corinthians 3:13-14). But our works will also be burned up like stubble (1 Corinthians 3:15) and we "shall suffer loss." I don't hear **that** preached about very much. A saved person can suffer loss, yet still be saved. There are streets paved with transparent gold in heaven, so whatever that reward is, it's not material stuff. Maybe it's closeness to Jesus. Maybe it's position. Maybe our mansion. Whatever it is, it's something that we really do want to *gain*. We do not want to suffer loss.

And what will be the criteria, according to Jesus' words above? "Whosoever therefore shall be ashamed of me and of **my words...**" The criteria here is whether we are ashamed or unashamed of Jesus and His words. Wow.

If we are ashamed of Jesus and of Jesus' words —and once you realize that the *entire Bible* is really Jesus, the Son of God's words, it will change your life— then Jesus Himself shall be ashamed of us!

It would really hurt my children if I ever told them I was ashamed of them. The couple of times I said I was "disappointed" nearly crushed them. So for "the Judge of all the earth" (Genesis 18:25), who knows our every weakness, to be "ashamed of" us, that would be devastating beyond imagination.

Perhaps that's why God promises more than once He will "wipe away every tear" (Isaiah 25:8; Revelation 7:17; 21:4).

Our own words will convict us and reveal our shame, if we have been ashamed of God and His words, the unadulterated Bible.

Matthew 12:37 "For by thy words thou shalt be justified, and by thy words thou shalt be condemned."

ITS PRESERVED WORDS OPEN US TO THE FATHER'S PROMISES. In John 14:23, "Jesus answered and said unto him, If a man love me, he will keep **my words**:"

But the Lord Jesus didn't stop there. Look at the promises that follow:

"...my Father will love him, and we will come unto him, and make our abode with him."

His words will not have any problem trying to work in you to change your life, because you love Him and His words! That's awesome! Do you have problems in your life? Love Him and His words! And they will be able to work actively in your life.

The Holy Ghost inside you will work in and out of you, because you submit. Not because you're perfect, but because you submit. You love Him.

But again, how can you keep God's words, if you don't know what they are? Why is what professors call "the most error-filled Bible" continuing to produce such godly and holiness-seeking fruit? How can they call it that? Can you get good fruit from a corrupt tree? I'll let Jesus answer that.

Matthew 7:18 "A good tree cannot bring forth evil fruit, neither can a corrupt tree bring forth good fruit."

PART 3 – THE SUPERIORITY OF THE KING JAMES BIBLE

Its History Shows That God Had A Plan.

Remember, I was turned away from the King James. I preached, from the pulpit, after I was ordained, that "The only thing worse than the King James was the Living Bible." The ONLY thing worse? Is it true? Or, is it that there's something about that old-fashioned, outdated, mistranslated-according-to-modern-standards Book, that, through its despised pages, outshines them all?

Could it be that they've made some mistake? Could our best supposedly scientific scholarship have missed something? Did they, in their quest to explain away the Bible, in its place create a Frankenstein's monster, into which they couldn't put life, no matter how hard they tried? "We have everything we need to create life." He says, "Great! Go into a graveyard and grab a bunch of pieces, stand them on the table there. Alright, put life into 'em!"

Having all the parts isn't enough, is it? You need the Spirit of God to be breathed into it.

Could God have had a plan so simple that it put all their brilliance to shame? Could the King James Bible be so effective because it's really His Book?

I tell people all the time, "This is not my Book. It's God's Book." I am asked: "Brother David, could you please make another Bible where you fix the words and just make them a little easier to understand?" I said, "I'm scared to death to do ANYTHING to this Book." I mean, with all my heart I believe it. Even if I made a million dollars, there is nothing, nothing that would make me feel worse than the idea that I had messed with what God said.

But if so, what WAS His plan?

Remember, we aren't God. So His plan doesn't have to

follow our rules. Let me give you a real quick run-through. And whatever His plan was, it worked already. It was done, past tense. Please remember that. We don't have to make it work. God already did that.

You see, there are a lot of people questioning what I'm about to tell you. But I'm saying we just have to look at the evidence and figure out what He did. I'm not standing at the beginning of history, saying these other Bibles are *going to* take away your faith. I'm standing at the **end** of history, reading the Bible analyses, and the surveys, and looking at the awful results in the churches, and telling you, "This has *already happened.*"

I'm not telling you that a 99% Bible *will perhaps* produce that result. I'm telling you a 99% Bible already *did*. That *IS* the result that came. We're at the end, not at the beginning. So this is the easiest job in the world to tell you this, because it's already happened.

And the very producers of those Bibles are telling me so. I've got their statistics. Think about the Fall of Man. The Devil really thought he had it made, didn't he? Here was the perfect man, the perfect woman:

"Adam, do you love me?"

"Who else?"

It was the perfect relationship.

Satan got in there and messed it up, somewhere in the first 120 years. Because at 130 years, Abel's gone, and Cain's in exile. That's when they started raising Seth. But somewhere in that first 120 years, the Devil finally got into that serpent, and spoke to Eve. And we're not going to get into all the details. But if you have your King James Bible and read Genesis 3, you know the rest of the story.

But you know that ultimately the woman got deceived. And

the man made a choice that he wanted the girl over God, at this point, which often happens, especially in seminary and Bible college. That's the Fall of Man.

But what did God do? Did He have a plan? Yes! Genesis 3:15: "And I will put enmity between thee and the woman, and between thy seed and her seed; it shall bruise thy head, and thou shalt bruise his heel."

A prophecy of the Christ, because He's "...the Lamb slain from the foundation of the world"!

And that prophecy shows that **God had a plan**. Wait. God had a plan? Yes, God had a plan!

So let's jump 4,000 years. What happened after Pentecost? Very early on in the church, the Devil gets into these people and starts organizing their church into a religion, and they start getting power in Antioch. Even though they gave us the word of God, they got the Bible encrusted with the *civitas*, the Roman ideas on community and government.

So you didn't have pastors, elders, deacons. You had bishops and archbishops and monarchical episcopates. Then they had higher people over them, and then eventually cardinals, and then popes. All that stuff built up, starting, like 100 AD. Even Ignatius of Antioch, at the place where the scriptures were gathered, got sucked into what became the Roman Catholic hierarchical form of government. The fact is, everybody became a mixed bag right after John died.

But God had a plan. Now when these guys, the Greek guys, as opposed to the Latin guys, got together, they debated, "What about Jesus Christ?" "What about this? What about that?" "Who do you baptize? Does that save?" And all sorts of other topics. Well, they were already thinking that it was a good idea to baptize babies. So Acts 8:37 had to go. They had a great way to take care of it: snip, snip, snip, toss! "***What*** Acts 8:37?"

Let me give you some background. In the Latin-speaking world, God had provided a translation of the Bible, which we call the Old Latin, translated by 157 AD. It was written for the common person, so it was a true "Vulgate," or Common Bible in Latin.

The Greeks had the words of God. But they started to have their own "emerging church" movement. But what eventually emerged was a compromised church. As they engaged in doctrinal debates, their solution was to change the Bible to fit their doctrine, not the other way around.

But at this time there were still Latin Bibles that were made before the Greeks started removing words. So even though the Greek scholars were taking words out of their Bibles, the Latin believers still had what God really said. On top of that, the Latin scholars didn't have the same debates. So they had no reason to remove Acts 8:37. But in the Greek-speaking world they went snip, snip, snip, toss! The Devil thought he had it made.

But God had a plan. Did God know where the right words were? Yes, He did! Remember at this time there were no publishing companies. There were simply hand-made copies, one at a time. So if you make a mistake, it's just one copy. But there were other copies in other places, that you can check.

And then finally they got to where they had a problem with the Father, the Word and the Holy Ghost. And different groups asked "Is God just one?" Patripassianism: did the Father suffer on the cross? Is the Father equal and identical to the Son? And what about this? What about that-- AAAH! 1 John 5:7-5:8a: snip, snip, snip, toss! "***What*** 1 John 5:7-5:8a?"

PART 3 – THE SUPERIORITY OF THE KING JAMES BIBLE

Other languages and groups, they still had those words. But they took it out of the Greek. Oh no! That's the end of the world! No, it's not, because…

God had a plan. By the time you get to the 1400s, 1453, in come the Muslims, and Constantinople falls to them. And the Greeks run away with their Bibles and their Greek manuscripts, and they run into the Latin world. And then the pope goes, "Uh oh. We don't have control over those Greek manuscripts. We've got to get somebody to learn to translate those documents."

And a priest named Erasmus starts learning Greek and going to libraries and finding manuscripts. The Roman Catholic religion had already changed the Latin Bible under Jerome, creating a Roman Catholic Latin Vulgate. Then they spent centuries trying to destroy all the real Old Latin translations of God's words. Now in the early 1500s, Erasmus uncovered in Church libraries Greek texts that were clearly the word of God. They were not corrupted, like the Catholic Latin Vulgate.

Erasmus realized that if he was going to make a New Testament, it needed to be from these uncorrupted copies of the Greek, and then make changes to the Latin New Testament as needed. So he decided to make a preserved text, parallel New Testament, Greek and Latin. But the pope, Leo X, would likely only endorse one, and another group was about to push their text for the pope's approval. Erasmus had to act fast.

Erasmus wrote a big, flattering note to the pope. He was so overjoyed by this dedication that he approved Erasmus' text ahead of the Catholic scholar's text. And so Erasmus got permission to publish what turned out to be the preserved Greek text, and a fixed Latin one in addition! Over the years he refined his work, but since his text was approved, now he could take his time smoothing it out.

It's awesome to think that, for a couple hundred years the Catholics were forced to use the *right* New Testament! That's why they were so desperate to stop it.[3] Thank you, Erasmus!

But God still had a plan. At the same time that Greeks were fleeing Constantinople, in the 1450s, a guy named Johannes Gutenberg perfected the movable type printing press in Mainz, Germany. Then we had a different thing happening in the world: multiple copies. He started with the Roman Catholic Latin Vulgate, hoping to make big bucks off of wealthy customers. Oops! Wrong Bible!

But God had a different plan. Adolph II invaded Mainz a few years later in 1462 and all the people sworn to secrecy grabbed parts of the press and went and made their own presses in other places. Printing presses spread all over the empire. It's awesome! Because God was preparing more of ***His plan.***

Then throughout the 1500s they started gathering together the preserved text. Erasmus' text showed up in Luther's church in 1516. A few years later Tyndale learned Greek in England. He knew 7 different languages. When he was denied permission to print in England, he went to Worms in Germany. His Greek manuscript, translated into English, became the start of the English translations. In the meantime, the Catholic church was trying to overrun them. BOOM! They wanted to destroy everything!!

But God had a plan. There was a little island across the English Channel that God was going to use. And finally in

---

[3] In response to the threat of the real Bible arose the orders of the Jesuits and Benedictine Maurists. See *Is the 'World's Oldest Bible' a Fake?* for more information.

PART 3 – THE SUPERIORITY OF THE KING JAMES BIBLE

1604-1611 He got together the right people, the right time, the right manuscripts, the right location, the right arrangement, the right idea of how to do it, so they had to all agree, no matter what their denominational differences, about God's words, not theirs. And then we got the King James Bible.

"Well, why does it have those odd words?"

"I don't care."

"Well, what about this or that argument?"

I don't care. God knew where all the right pieces were. There's no tricking God. He knows what's in His book. He knows what He said.

GOD KNEW WHERE EVERYTHING WAS. He just needed to put it together for the End Time. I really believe God knew —His being God and all— that English was going to be a "World Language," spoken in many nations. It would be the "End Time" language that God would use in the greatest missionary effort in all history to spread His Word throughout the world. "And then shall the end come." (Matt. 24:14) This KJV is the End Time Bible.

There are all sorts of different translations, that come from English! This is the End Time language. What's the language of the internet? English. Some claim there are more English speakers in China than almost any country of the world. So let me end with this:

God had a plan.

Jeremiah 29:11 "For I know the thoughts that I think toward you, saith the LORD, thoughts of peace, and not of evil, to give you an expected end."

The King James Bible is God's words preserved in English, in a Book. It's His book.

God wants, in the End Times, for us to have multiple

millions and billions of copies of His words. And then any other translation that matches by meaning and proper phrasing and grammatical structure in their language, to these words —because these words are God's words— will also be God's words.

Trust God's plan.

Trust His holy and preserved words in English, the King James Bible.

Trust the superior Bible. God will reward you, both in this life, and in the life to come. You have ***His word*** on it.

PART 4 – Here's How

In the previous sections of this book you have learned that the notion that the King James Bible is too hard to read is a myth.

You have also learned the many reasons why you should read God's words in classic English instead of the defective modern versions.

Part four contains some practical suggestions for reading the King James. Also included is a dictionary of the less familiar words in the classic English of the KJV and some helpful charts of biblical weights and measures.

A 30-Day Challenge

As the preceding chapters illustrate, the King James is not too hard to read. But it does take some practice to get started. I challenge you to read it out loud each day for 30 days. Give it a full 30 days. Anything that really matters that much —it's purporting to be your guide for your life, your personal owner's manual, from your God— is worth 30 days to check it out.

When you read this book and you pray to the Author Who wrote it, He will teach you so many things. You can move forward in your faith and He can bring blessings to you in your life. It's worth it. **Take the 30-day challenge.**

The 5-Ribbon Plan

The Lord's Prayer has the words, "Give us this day our daily bread" (Matthew 6:11).

Jesus isn't just talking about food. As Jesus said, "Man shall not live by bread alone, but by every word that proceedeth out of the mouth of God" (Matthew 4:4).

We need a steady diet of God's words. But how do we penetrate what seems like a "closed Book" to many?

God meant His words to be read, prayed over, thought about, and acted upon. That means His words can change us any day of the week (not just Sunday).

Here are some ways God provided for us to open His book and dive right in, at any time.

Do not be afraid if you cannot write a doctoral dissertation on the dispensations of grace. God never meant it to be that hard! He wanted ordinary people like us to pray to Him for understanding and start reading at any point.

Here are five easy sections to our Bible. If we read just a bit from each section every day, we will start learning about our God and what He wants us to know.

1. Old Testament History:
Genesis through Esther

God shows us His interactions with man from the creation of the universe to the Hebrews' return from the Babylonian Captivity and rebuilding (sort of) of the temple in Jerusalem. God doesn't change. How He interacted with people then is pretty much how He will interact with us now. We learn a lot about God's character when we pay attention to these important lessons.

2. Wisdom Literature:
Job through Song of Solomon

God teaches us a major theme: The fear of the LORD is the beginning of wisdom. After we fear God, there are many principles we can learn from God's storehouse of wisdom that He is waiting to pour out on us (See Proverbs 2).

3. Prophets:
Isaiah through Malachi

God sent His representatives to turn His people back to Him, to show them their sins and His righteousness, and to tell them about His future plans for the world and for His people. This shows us that God means what He says and will accomplish what He promises. The prophets teach us more about what is dear to God's heart, how jealous He is for His people, and that He keeps his promises!

4. New Testament History:
Matthew through Acts

The Gospels show us God in action on the earth, in the Person of the Son of God, the Lord Jesus Christ. His tenderness and mercy, and His warnings of judgment, are all contained in four easy-to-read Gospels. The Acts are the continuation of what Christ started, first through His apostles and then through the believers, as they began to act upon Jesus' command to teach Jerusalem, Judea, Samaria, and the ends of the earth.

5. The Epistles:
Romans through Revelation

Epistles is another word for "letters." These are written to God's people. Some are addressed to churches, and others to specific individuals. God packed a lifetime of powerful instructions within these 22 books. Learn how God wants us to conduct our lives and manage His church. Begin with prayer and see what the Lord helps you learn!

* * *

Here's a way to keep track of this new reading plan that I've found helpful.

I use 5 ribbons for the five sections, and color-code them to remind me quickly what each section is about:
1. Old Testament History: Purple, the color of royalty
2. Wisdom Literature: Green, for growth
3. Old Testament Prophets: Rose, the mixture of red and white, judgment mixed with mercy
4. New Testament History: Red, for the blood of the Lord Jesus Christ
5. The Epistles: Blue, like the sky and the waters of life, the letters to prepare us for heaven.

Here's how you can make your own Bible ribbons:

Step 1:

Using white glue, assemble ordinary cardboard stock, and five 3mm or 6mm ribbons like this:

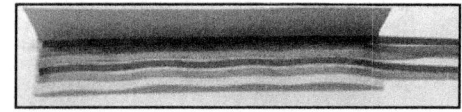

Place them in this order: Purple, Green, Rose, Red, Blue.

Step 2:

Insert your folded, glued, dried bookmark into the spine of your Bible.

Step 3:

Set each bookmark in Chapter 1 of its section: purple in Genesis, green in Job, rose in Isaiah, red in Matthew and blue in Romans. Each day as you read a chapter, move the ribbon forward to keep your place.

Note: To keep your Bible ribbons from fraying, you may want to coat the ends with a little clear nail polish.

The Proverbs Reading Plan

It turns out I'm not the only one who does this. I was amazed to find out many have grown in their faith and how to make good decisions by following this simple program. Ready?

Every month has no more than 31 days. Proverbs has 31 chapters. At any time, we can look at the calendar and see which day it is. Then we can grab that chapter of Proverbs and start reading. It's that simple!

No bookmark necessary. We are never lost on what to read. What if you forgot to read yesterday? Don't beat yourself up about it. Read today's reading. Then if you want to after that, look at the one(s) you missed. This is low-pressure, but high yield. The Proverbs have helped me to make so many good decisions from the day I started this reading plan, that I have no intention to stop, no matter what other readings I may do.

Appendix

Why Do We Need "Thee" and "Thou"?

In almost every language but modern English, people know whether the speaker is addressing one person or many. In Classical English, if the speaker is talking to one person, he uses "thee" or "thou." If he is talking to many people, he says "you" or "your." The King James preserves this. Jesus said to Nicodemus, "Marvel not that I said unto thee (Nicodemus), ye (all of you people) must be born again" (John 3:7). Jesus was telling Nicodemus that all people of all times must be born again! A very important doctrine that is lost without "thee" and "thou."

It takes only a single generation to make a word archaic... and a single generation of Bible readers can bring it back into use. —David W. Daniels

The King James Bible Companion
A listing of over 600 archaic words defined.

Where there is more than one meaning for a word, the one that applies will be apparent by the context of the verse. It is common that words have more than one meaning, depending on the way they are used. No attempt is made here to provide every possible meaning, but rather to give the meaning that applies to its usage in the Scriptures

Abase *Make or bring low; to humble* .... Job 40:11
Abated *Reduced in intensity or amount* .... Genesis 8:3
Abhor *Despise; spurn; regard with horror* .... Exodus 5:21

Abjects *People thrown out; outcasts* .... Psalms 35:15
Abode *To have stayed; remained; a dwelling* .... Genesis 29:14
Acceptation *Acceptance; approval* .... 1 Timothy 1:15; 4:9
Acquit *Judged not guilty* .... Job 10:14
Adamant *Rock or very hard mineral* .... Ezekiel 3:9
Adjure *To command, under oath or threat* .... Joshua 6:26
Ado *Fuss; bother; tumult* .... Mark 5:39
Advertise *To advise; warn; inform; reveal* .... Numbers 24:14
Advisement *Counsel; consideration* .... 1 Chronicles 12:19
Affinity *Become a son-in-law; an in-law* .... 1 Kings 3:1
Affording *Providing; yielding (as of crops)* .... Psalms 144:13
Affright *To frighten* .... Deuteronomy 7:21
Afoot *On foot* .... Mark 6:33
Afore *Before* .... 2 Kings 20:4
Afresh *Again; anew* .... Hebrews 6:6
Agone *Ago* .... 1 Samuel 30:13
Ague *A fever* .... Leviticus 26:16
Alamoth *Treble instruments; woman singers;
            music played in treble (high notes)* .... 1 Chronicles 15:20
Albeit *"Although it be that," shortened* .... Ezekiel 13:7
All to *To do entirely; do wholly* .... Judges 9:53
Alleluia *"Praise ye the LORD!"* .... Revelation 19:1
Allow *To approve; commend; accept* .... Luke 11:48
Alms *Giving to the poor to help them* .... Matthew 6:1 ff.
Aloof *At a distance, but within view* .... Psalms 38:11
Ambassage *Ambassador(s); a message* .... Luke 14:32
Ambushment *Attack by surprise; ambush* .... 2 Chronicles 13:13
Amerce *To punish by imposing a fine* .... Deuteronomy 22:19
Amiable *Dear; lovely; beloved* .... Psalms 84:1
Amiss *Wrong; incorrect* .... 2 Chronicles 6:37

APPENDIX

Anathema *To be damned by God* . . . . 1 Corinthians 16:22
Angle *Fishhook* . . . . Isaiah 19:8
Anise *Plant of the parsley family.* . . . . Matthew 23:23
Anon *Immediately; right away* . . . . Matthew 13:20
Apace *At a quick pace; quickly.* . . . . 2 Samuel 18:25
Apothecary *One who makes perfumes.* . . . . Exodus 30:25
Appertain *To belong to; to pertain to.* . . . . Leviticus 6:5
Ariel *"Lion of God," name for Jerusalem.* . . . . Isaiah 29:1-2, 7
Ark *The ship Noah built; box; chest;* . . . . Genesis 6:14;
  the basket boat of baby Moses . . . . Exodus 2:3
Array *To put on; to clothe.* . . . . Genesis 41:42
Art *You (one person) are* . . . . Genesis 3:9
Artificer *Artisan; craftsman.* . . . . Genesis 4:22
Artillery *War equipment; weapons.* . . . . 1 Samuel 20:40
Asp *Snake; serpent* . . . . Deuteronomy 32:33
Assayed *Attempted; tested; analyzed.* . . . . Deuteronomy 4:34
Assent *Accord; agreement.* . . . . 2 Chronicles 18:12
Asswage *Lessen; relieve; satisfy; sweeten* . . . . Genesis 8:1
Astonied *Be taken by surprise* . . . . Ezra 9:3-4
Asunder *Apart; into separate parts* . . . . Leviticus 1:17
Atonement *A person or animal taking another's*
  place, to cover sins . . . . Exodus 29:33
Attent *Attentive; observant.* . . . . 2 Chronicles 6:40
Augment *Increase; make bigger* . . . . Numbers 32:14
Austere *Severe; strict; harsh; solemn* . . . . Luke 19:21-22
Averse *Disliking; turned from* . . . . Micah 2:8
Avouched *Affirmed; admitted; vouched for* . . . . . Deuteronomy 26:17-18
Away with *OT: To tolerate; bear; endure.* . . . . Isaiah 1:13;
  NT: "Take away!" . . . . Luke 23:18
Axletree *Spindle/shaft on which a wheel rotates* . . . . 1 Kings 7:32-33.
Backbiting *Evil speaking; slandering.* . . . . Psalms 15:3

Balm *A medicine; rosin from a bush*..................Genesis 37:25
Banquetings *Drinking, gluttony; rich partying*............1 Peter 4:3
Baptize *Immerse; dip a thing*........................Matthew 3:6
Barbarous *Foreign*....................................Acts 28:2
Barked *Scraped the bark off*...........................Joel 1:7
Base (to be) *Low; lowly; humble*...................2 Samuel 6:22
Battlement *Low wall around a roof*.............Deuteronomy 22:8
          Wall for defense........................Jeremiah 5:10
Became him *Was fitting for; was exactly suited for*...Hebrews 2:10; 7:26
Beeves *Cattle*....................................Leviticus 22:19
Begat, beget *To be father of; be ancestor of*........Genesis 4:18; 17:20
Behemoth *A large, plant-eating dragon or dinosaur*........Job 40:15 ff.
Belied *Lied against; spoken falsely*....................Jeremiah 5:12
Beseech *To call upon; appeal; beg*......................Exodus 3:18
Besom *Broom*.......................................Isaiah 14:23
Besought *Asked the favor of; searched for*...............Genesis 42:21
Beset *To surround; to entangle*............Judges 19:22; Hebrews 12:1
Bestead *See "hardly bestead."*..........................Isaiah 8:21
Bestow *Give; grant; put; place*......................Exodus 32:29
          Store; gather together in one place..............Luke 12:17-18
Bethink *Come to one's senses, consider*..................1 Kings 8:47
Betimes *Early; in good time; before it's too late*...........Genesis 26:31
Betwixt *Between; passing from one to another*...........Genesis 17:11
Bewail *To express deep sorrow; lament*.....Leviticus 10:6; Jeremiah 4:31
Bewray *Reveal; give away a secret; betray*..............Proverbs 27:16
Billow *A great wave or swelling of water*.................Psalms 42:7
Bishoprick *Guardianship; office of overseeing*..............Acts 1:20
Blains *Blisters; sores; boils*..........................Exodus 9:9-10
Blaze *To make known; proclaim*.......................Mark 1:45
Bolled *Blossomed; in the seed or pod*...................Exodus 9:31
Bolster *Pillow; head (or other) support*................1 Samuel 19:13

Bondman *A slave; an unpaid worker* . . . . Genesis 44:33
Bosses *Bump-like shapes on a shield*. . . . . Job 15:26
Botch *An ulcer, swelling, tumor*. . . . . Deuteronomy 28:27, 35
Bowels *Inward parts; affections* . . . . Genesis 15:4
Brawler *One who gets into fights* . . . . 1 Timothy 3:3; Titus 3:2
Bray a fool *Beat, bruise, pound on a fool*. . . . . Proverbs 27:22
Bray *Groan, wail; make a foul noise*. . . . . Job 6:5; 30:7
Breach *Breaking forth; a break;*
    opening, inlet. . . . . . Genesis 38:29, Leviticus 24:20, Judges 5:17
Breeches *Trousers* . . . . Exodus 28:42
Brigandine *Armor for a soldier or robber* . . . . Jeremiah 46:4; 51:3
Brimstone *Sulfur*. . . . . Genesis 19:24
Broided *Braided; plaited; interweaved* . . . . 1 Timothy 2:9
Broidered *Embroidered; adorned with needlework*. . . . . Exodus 28:4
Brood *Animal offspring, especially of birds* . . . . Luke 13:34
Bruit *Report; rumor; sound; noise*. . . . . Jeremiah 10:22
Brutish *Stupid as a beast; slow to understand*. . . . . Psalms 49:10
Buckler *Round shield held with a grip* . . . . Psalms 18:30
Buffet *To strike with a clenched fist* . . . . Matthew 26:67
Bulrush *Tall plant near water, such as papyrus*. . . . . Exodus 2:3
Bulwark *A defensive structure* . . . . Deuteronomy 20:20
Bunches of camels *Camels' humps* . . . . Isaiah 30:6
By and by *At once; immediately; soon* . . . . Matthew 13:21
Caldron *A pot; kettle; cauldron*. . . . . 1 Samuel 2:14
Canker *Something that eats away, corrodes;*
    cancer; gangrene; an ulcer-like sore. . . . . 2 Timothy 2:17
Carbuncle *A red precious stone* . . . . Exodus 28:17
Careful *Full of care; full of worry, anxiety*. . . . . Jeremiah 17:8
Carnal *Of the flesh, fleshly; sensual*. . . . . 1 Corinthians 3:3
Carriage *That which is carried; baggage*. . . . . Judges 18:21
Casement *A window* . . . . Proverbs 7:6

Cast angle *To fish with a hook* .... Isaiah 19:8
Cast in the teeth *Revile or reproach, face to face.* .... Matthew 27:44
Caul *Membrane; fatty tissue around a bodily organ* .... Exodus 29:13
Cauls *Close-fitting caps/nets worn by women.* .... Isaiah 3:18
Celestial *Relating to the sky or heavens.* .... 1 Corinthians 15:40
Centurion *Roman commander of a hundred men* .... Matthew 8:5
Chambering *Sexual indulgence; lewdness* .... Romans 13:13
Chamberlain *Eunuch or chief servant;*
one in charge of the king's quarters. .... 2 Kings 23:11
Chamois *A small sheep-like antelope* .... Deuteronomy 14:5
Champaign *A plain; field; flat, open land.* .... Deuteronomy 11:30
Chapiter *Upper part of a column or pillar.* .... Exodus 36:38
Chapmen *Tradesmen; merchants.* .... 2 Chronicles 9:14
Chargeable *A burden; an undue weight* .... 2 Samuel 13:25
Charger *A large platter or dish* .... Numbers 7:13
Charity *Godly love in action* .... 1 Corinthians 8:1; 13:1-4
Chaste *Pure; clean; not corrupt* .... 2 Corinthians 11:2
Check *Rebuke; reproof; stop an action* .... Job 20:3
Chide *Quarrel; scold; complain; find fault* .... Exodus 17:2
Choler *Anger, wrath* .... Daniel 8:7; 11:11
Churl *A rude, harsh person* .... Isaiah 32:5, 7
Cieled *Covered on the inside of a roof/room* .... 2 Chronicles 3:5
Circumspect (be) *Be watchful every way; take heed.* ..... Exodus 23:13
Clamour *Yelling; loud complaining* .... Ephesians 4:31
Cleanness of teeth *Famine.* .... Amos 4:6
Cleave *Split open; cut open; divide.* .... Leviticus 1:17
Cleave unto *Cling to; hold to; stick to.* .... Genesis 2:24
Cleft *Split hoof; an opening, break or split* .... Deuteronomy 14:6
Clouts *Pieces of cloth used to patch.* .... Jeremiah 38:11 f.
Cloven *Separated; split; divided up* .... Deuteronomy 14:7

APPENDIX

Coast *Border; region/country; land by water* . . . . Exodus 10:14
Cockatrice *Venomous snake* . . . . Isaiah 11:8
Cockle *A weed resembling wheat* . . . . Job 31:40
Cogitations *Thinking something over* . . . . Daniel 7:28
Collop *A piece of flesh or fold of fat* . . . . Job 15:27
Comely *Attractive; proper; becoming* . . . . 1 Samuel 16:18
Communicate *(When not referring to speech)*
 share; give; associate with . . . . Galatians 6:6
Compass *Go around, encircle; encompass*. . . . . .Genesis 2:11
Concision *Those who believe circumcision makes*
 one righteous or saves . . . . Philippians 3:2
Concord *Agreement; unison* .2 Corinthians 6:15
Concupiscence *Strong lust; passion* . . . . Romans 7:8
Confectionary *Perfume/ointment maker; perfumer*. . . . . . 1 Samuel 8:13
Consecrate *Treat as set apart or separate unto God* . . . . Exodus 28:3
Constantly *Firmly; consistently;*
 continually. . . . . 1 Chronicles 28:7; Proverbs 21:28
Constrain *Compel with irresistible force* . . . . 2 Kings 4:8
Consumption *Disease that eats the body;*
 destruction . . . . Leviticus 26:16; Isaiah 10:22
Contemn *Despise with mockery; show contempt*. . . . . Psalms 10:13
Contentious *Loving to quarrel and angrily debate*. . . . . . . Proverbs 21:19
Convenient *Fit; appropriate; proper* . . . . Proverbs 30:8
Conversation *Behavior; way of life; community* . . . . Psalms 37:14
Convince *Convict; prove wrong*. . . . . Job 32:12
Coping *Top of a wall, sloped to drain off water* . . . . 1 Kings 7:9
Corn *Any kind of edible grain* . . . . .Genesis 27:28
Cornet *A wind instrument; horn; trumpet* . . . . 2 Samuel 6:5
Cotes *Animal enclosures; stables* . . . . .2 Chronicles 32:28
Coulter *Sharp iron blade on the front of a plow,*
 that cuts into the soil. . . . . 1 Samuel 13:20

Countenance *Face, appearance; show favor.* . . . Genesis 4:5; Exodus 23:3
Countervail *Be or make equal; compensate* . . . . Esther 7:4
Covert *A shelter; a hiding place* . . . . 1 Samuel 25:20
Cracknels *Dry, brittle cakes or biscuits* . . . . 1 Kings 14:3
Crisping pins *Pins heated up to curl hair; curling irons* . . . . . Isaiah 3:22
Cruse *A pot.* . . . . 1 Samuel 26:11
Cumbered *To be overwhelmed with cares* . . . . Luke 10:40
Cummin *A plant bearing aromatic seeds* . . . . Isaiah 28:25
Curious *Skillfully made; detailed.* . . . . Exodus 28:8
Curious arts *Divination; sorcery; astrology* . . . . Acts 19:19
Dam *A mother.* . . . . Exodus 22:30
Daub *To cover or plaster.* . . . . Exodus 2:3; Ezekiel 13:10
Daysman *A judge; mediator; "umpire."* . . . . Job 9:33
Dayspring *Sunrise* . . . . Job 38:12
Dearth *A drought; famine; no harvest* . . . . Genesis 41:54
Defer *Delay; postpone* . . . . Genesis 34:19
Derision *Ridicule; laughing at enemies' threats.* . . . . Job 30:1
Descry *Search out; map out; to describe* . . . . Judges 1:23
Despite *Contempt; angry hatred* . . . . Ezekiel 25:6
Diadem *Royal headband worn by Eastern kings* . . . . Job 29:14
Discomfited *Defeated in battle; scattered* . . . . Exodus 17:13
Discover *Uncover; reveal; have first sight of* . . . . Exodus 20:26
Disdain *To despise; to reject.* . . . . 1 Samuel 17:42
Dissembled *Used deceit; pretended; feigned.* . . . . Joshua 7:11
Dissimulation *Hypocrisy; create false appearances* . . . . Romans 12:9
Divers *Old spelling of "diverse;" unequal* . . . . Proverbs 20:10
Doleful *Mournful cry; sorrowful howl* . . . . Isaiah 13:21
Dragon *Huge lizard; dinosaur.* . . . . Deuteronomy 32:33;
The Devil; Satan . . . . Rev 12:9
Draught house *Public toilet* . . . . 2 Kings 10:27

Draught of fish *Fish caught by sweeping a net* . . . . .Luke 5:9

Dregs *Grounds at the bottom of a cup* . . . . Psalms 75:8

Dropsy *An illness where a part or all of
the body swells with too much water* . . . . .Luke 14:2

Drove (n.) *Flock; a company*. . . . . .Genesis 32:16

Duke *Head of a family or tribe* . . . . Genesis 36:15 ff.

Durst *He/she dared; was bold enough*. . . . . .Esther 7:5

Earing *Plowing; tilling the ground*. .Genesis 45:6

Earnest (n.) *Down payment*. .2 Corinthians 1:22

Effeminate *Acting like a woman; unmanly* . . . . .1 Corinthians 6:9

Emerods *Hemorrhoids; tumors* . . . . 1 Samuel 5:6

Emulation *Trying to equal or be better than others* . . . . . .Romans 11:14;
(in either a good or bad way). . . . . Galatians 5:20

Enjoin *Command; charge* . . . . .Esther 9:31

Enmity *Hatred, being an enemy* . . . . Genesis 3:15, Lk 23:12

Ensample *Example; pattern or model to imitate*. . . . . .1 Corinthians 10:11

Ensign *Flag or banner, as of an army*. . . . . Numbers 2:2

Ensue *Pursue; to follow after* . . . . 1 Peter 3:11

Environ *Surround; compass*. . . . . Joshua 7:9

Ephah *About 6/10 bushel;*. . . . . Exodus 16:36;
a basket holding that amount . . . . Zechariah 5:6-10

Ephod *Linen garment worn by the high priest* . . . . . Exodus 25:7; 28:6 ff.

Epistle *Important or formal letter*. . . . . 1 Thes 5:27

Ere *Before; until*. . . . . .Exodus 1:19

Eschew *Avoid; shun; turn aside from* . . . . 1 Peter 3:11

Espied *Discovered; spied out; examined* . . . . .Genesis 42:27

Euroclydon *Furious, north-easterly wind*. . . . . Acts 27:14

Even, eveningtide *Evening time* . . . . .Genesis 19:1

Every several *Every single; each one separately*. . . . . . .2 Chronicles 11:12

Exactors *Overseers; tribute or tax collectors*. . . . . Isaiah 60:17

Exhortation *Encouragement; counsel*. . . . . .1 Corinthians 14:3

Extol *To lift up; to praise; to esteem.* . . . . Psalms 30:1
Eyesalve *Medicine for the eyes* . . . . Revelation 3:18
Fain *Earnestly want to or long to; gladly* . . . . Job 27:22
Fairs *Something gotten at a fair; wares* . . . . Ezekiel 27:12 ff.
Fan *Winnowing fan; a fork-shaped tool
to throw grain in the air, to let the wind
separate the wheat from the chaff.* . . . . Isaiah 30:24
Fast *Abstaining from food.* . . . . Matthew 6:16-18
Fatling *Fat cattle.* . . . . 1 Samuel 15:9
Fats *Vats (always plural: "fats")* . . . . Joel 2:24; 3:13
Feign *To pretend to be; To disguise* . . . . 1 Samuel 21:13
Felloe *The rim of a wheel, held by spokes* . . . . 1 Kings 7:33
Fens *Marshes; swamps* . . . . Job 40:21
Fetched a compass *Went on a circular course* . . . . Joshua 15:3
Fillet *An ornamental band around the top of
a pillar; a thin band or strip* . . . . Exodus 27:10
Firebrand *Burning wood; a torch* . . . . Judges 15:4
Firkin *About 9 gallons (40 liters) of liquid* . . . . John 2:6
Firmament *Expanse or vault over the earth; sky;
the stretched-out heavens.* . . . . Genesis 1:6-8
Fitches *A kind of grain used for seasoning.* . . . . Isaiah 28:25, 27
Flagon *Bottle holding liquid; flask; an amount
equal to what a flagon holds.* . . . . 2 Samuel 6:19
Flay *Strip the skin off an animal or person* . . . . Micah 3:3
Flowers (her) *Menstrual flow; a woman's period* . . . . Leviticus 15:24
Flux *Bloody flow from the body; dysentery* . . . . Acts 28:8
Fold *Times (multiply, e.g., "twofold" = x2)* . . . . Genesis 4:15
Forbear *Refrain; restrain; refrain from acting* . . . . Exodus 23:5
Foresaw *Saw or knew beforehand* . . . . Acts 2:25
Forswear *Swear falsely; Commit perjury.* . . . . Matthew 5:33

APPENDIX

Forwardness,
be forward *Being eager; zealous; ready;*
being inclined to do something. . . . . .2 Corinthians 8:8
Foursquare *Squared; four cornered* .Exodus 27:1
Fray *Frighten; make afraid* .Deuteronomy 28:26
Fret *Be grieved; be troubled; be displeased* . . . . 1 Samuel 1:6
Fretting *Eating away; wearing away* . . . . Leviticus 13:51 ff.
Froward *Perverse; twisted* . . . . .Deuteronomy 32:20
Fuller *Washer and/or bleacher of clothes* . . . . Mark 9:3
Furbish *Rub, scour or polish until bright* . . . . .Jeremiah 46:4
Furlong *Approximately 1/8 mile (660 feet)* . . . . .Luke 24:13
Gaddest about *Go back and forth, to and fro* . . . . .Jeremiah 2:36
Gainsay *Contradict; oppose* . . . . .Luke 21:15
Gall *Something bitter or poisonous* . . . . .Deuteronomy 32:32
Garrison *Fortification; military post* . . . . 1 Samuel 10:5
Gin *Noose; snare* . . . . .Job 18:9
Girdle, Girt *Belt, wrapped around* . . . . Mark 1:6; 2 Kings 1:8
Go to *Come; let us begin (exhortation)* . . . . .Genesis 11:3
Grave *Tomb (noun); engraved (verb);* . . . . . . .Genesis 35:20; Exodus 28:9
serious, not showy (adj) . . . . 1 Timothy 3:8
Graven *Carved or engraved idol or image* . . . . .Exodus 20:4
Grisled *Spotted; speckled* . . . . .Genesis 31:10
Grove *Small group of trees; in pagan use,*
a place where Ashtaroth was worshiped . . . . Genesis 21:33;
(compare Judges 2:13 with 3:7) . . . . .Exodus 34:13
Guile *Deceit; craftiness* . . . . .Exodus 21:14
Habergeon *Coat of mail for the neck (and down)* . . . . .Exodus 28:32
Haft *A handle* . . . . Judges 3:22
Hale *Drag; force* . . . . .Luke 12:58
Halt *Lame; crippled in the feet* . . . . Matthew 18:8
Hap (Her hap was to) *To happen (She happened to.)* . . . . .Ruth 2:3

Haply *Perhaps; maybe* .... 1 Samuel 14:30
Hard by *Beside; next to* .... 1 Kings 21:1
Hardly bestead *Badly treated; greatly troubled* .... Isaiah 8:21
Harrow *Plow; break up clods; cover seed.* .... 2 Samuel 12:31
Hart *A stag; male deer* .... Deuteronomy 12:15
Haughty *Proud; arrogant; lifted up* .... 2 Samuel 22:28
Haunt *Where one goes frequently* .... 1 Samuel 23:22
Heady *Headstrong; reckless; hasty* .... 2 Timothy 3:4
Heath *Small shrub found in open wastelands* .... Jeremiah 17:6
Heed *Pay attention; watch out* .... Genesis 31:24
Helm *Rudder and tiller to steer a ship.* .... James 3:4
Henceforth *From this time forth; from now on* .... Genesis 4:12
Hereafter *After this; in time to come* ..... Isaiah 41:23; Revelation 9:12
Hereby *By this* .... Genesis 42:15; 1 John 4:13
Herein *In this* .... Genesis 34:22; 1 John 4:17
Hereof *Of this; from this* .... Matthew 9:26; Hebrews 5:3
Heretofore *Before now; in times past;
              formerly* .... Exodus 4:10; 2 Corinthians 13:2
Hereunto *Unto this* .... Eccl 2:25; 1 Peter 2:21
Herewith *With this* .... Ezekiel 16:29; Malachi 3:10
Hewn *Cut.* .... Exodus 20:25
Hinder end *The back side; behind; the rear.* .... 2 Samuel 2:23
Hireling *A hired laborer; employee.* .... Job 7:1
Hither, hitherto *To this place; till this point in time.* ...... Genesis 15:16
Hoar, hoary *White colored;
              white or gray with age* ..... Exodus 16:14; Leviticus 19:32
Holden *Held.* .... 2 Kings 23:22
Holpen *Helped.* .... Psalms 83:8
Hosen *Garments covering legs; trousers* .... Daniel 3:21
Host *Army/multitude; entertainer of guests* ...... Genesis 2:1; Luke 10:35
Hough *Hamstring; cut the tendons of the ham* .... Joshua 11:6, 9

APPENDIX

Husbandman *Farmer; one who tills the ground* ....Genesis 9:20
Ignominy *Contempt; shame; dishonor*................. Proverbs 18:3
Immutable *Unchangeable (an attribute of God)* ....Hebrews 6:18
Implacable *Cannot be calmed or appeased* .... Romans 1:31
Implead *Sue someone at law* .... Acts 19:38
Importunity *Urgent, continual, persistent asking*............Luke 11:8
Impotent *Weak; without strength or power* ....John 5:3
Impudent *Shameless; without modesty*................. Proverbs 7:13
Impute *Charge to one's account; reckon* ....Leviticus 7:18
In no wise *By no means; assuredly not*.................Leviticus 7:24
Incontinent *Without self-control; unbridled* .... 2 Timothy 3:3
Inditing *Dictating what to write*...................... Psalms 45:1
Inordinate *Unrestrained; immoderate*................. Ezekiel 23:11
Instant (adj.) *Insistent; persistent; importunate*............Luke 23:23
Issue *What comes forth: children;* .... Genesis 48:6;
  discharge of liquid...........................Leviticus 12:7
Jangling *Noisy argument; quarreling*................. 1 Timothy 1:6
Joined hard *Bordered; was adjacent to* .... Acts 18:7
Jot *The smallest Hebrew letter, yodh* .... Matthew 5:18
Kin, kindred *Family*...............................Leviticus 18:6
Kine *Cows; cattle*.................................Genesis 32:15
Knop *Knob; bud (as of a flower)* .... Exodus 25:33
Lade *To load; burden*..............................Genesis 45:17
Lasciviousness *Being lustful, loose or lewd;*
  promoting lustful desires in others .... Mark 7:22
Latchet *Sandal lace*................................. Isaiah 5:27
Laver *Wash basin*.................................Exodus 30:18
Leasing *Falsehood; deceit; lying* .... Psalms 4:2
Lees *Sediment settled in liquid; the dregs;* .... Jeremiah 48:11;
  (See "wines on the lees") ....Isaiah 25:6
Let (was let) *Hinder or obstruct*..................... Romans 1:13

Leviathan *Big dragon/dinosaur that lives near* .... Job 41:1 ff.;
   or in the water/sea .... Psalms 74:14.
Light off *To descend from; climb down from* .... Genesis 24:64
Light on, upon *To happen to find;*
   fall upon; hit. ..... Genesis 28:11; Deuteronomy 19:5
Lintel *Top of a door frame* .... Exodus 12:22-23
Listed, listeth *Choose; be inclined to do* .... Matthew 17:12
Lively *OT: Strong; energetic. NT: Living* .... Exodus 1:19; Acts 7:38
Loins *Thigh and groin area;*
   often used for the reproductive organs .... Genesis 35:11
Lot (one's) *Portion; what is received by casting lots* ... Deuteronomy 32:9
Lot (to cast) *Pebbles thrown to make decisions* .... Leviticus 16:8
Lowring *Threatening a storm; gloomy; clouded.* .... Matthew 16:3
Lucre *Gain in money or goods; profit* .... 1 Samuel 8:3
Lusty *Healthy and strong; able of body* .... Judges 3:29
Mammon *Earthly goods; property; riches* .... Matthew 6:24
Mantle *Cloak; covering garment* .... Judges 4:18
Maranatha *"Our Lord cometh."* .... 1 Corinthians 16:22
Marishes *Marshes; ponds.* .... Ezekiel 47:11
Matrix *A mother's womb* .... Exodus 13:12
Mattock *Hoe or other tool to break up dirt* .... 1 Samuel 13:20
Maul *Mallet, heavy hammer or club.* .... Proverbs 25:18
Maw *Animal's stomach.* .... Deuteronomy 18:3
Mean man *Common; low in rank.* .... Proverbs 22:29
Meat *Grain or food in general*
   (except where the verse refers to flesh) .... Genesis 1:29
Meet *Suitable; agreeable; fit; proper* .... Genesis 2:18
Mess *Portion of food* .... Genesis 43:34
Mete *Measure; deal out* .... Exodus 16:18
Meteyard *A rod to measure length; yardstick* .... Leviticus 19:35
Milch *Milk-giving; milking* .... Genesis 32:15

APPENDIX

Mincing *Taking short, quick steps* .... Isaiah 3:16
Minish *Diminish; lessen* .... Exodus 5:19
Ministration *Service; ministry* .... Luke 1:23
Mirth *Gladness; rejoicing* .... Genesis 31:27
Mite *Coin of very small value; 1/4 Denarius* .... Mark 12:42
Mitre *Turban; ceremonial headdress* .... Exodus 28:4
Mollified *Be softened; be appeased* .... Isaiah 1:6
Mortify *Put to death; remove the life of* .... Romans 8:13
Mote *Speck or splinter; small particle* .... Matthew 7:3-5
Muffler *Scarf or veil to cover the face* .... Isaiah 3:19
Munition *Stronghold; fort* .... Isaiah 29:7
Murrain *Cattle disease; pestilence; plague* .... Exodus 9:3
Naught *Bad; nothing; vain* .... 2 Kings 2:19; Proverbs 20:14
Nave *Hub; where spokes are inserted* .... 1 Kings 7:33
Necromancer *One who inquires of the dead* .... Deuteronomy 18:11
Neesings *Sneezing* .... Job 41:18
Nether *Lower* .... Exodus 19:17
Nigh *Near, in place or in time* .... Genesis 47:29
Nitre *Sodium nitrate, as in gunpowder* .... Proverbs 25:20
Noisome *Destructive; hurtful; noxious* .... Psalms 91:3
Not a whit *Not the least bit* .... 2 Corinthians 11:5
Nought *Nothing* .... Genesis 29:15
Obeisance *Bowing or kneeling in respect* .... Genesis 37:7
Odd number *What is left over; over and above* .... Numbers 3:48
Offend *Make angry; make one stumble; violate* .... Genesis 20:9
Offscouring *What is scoured off; rejected* .... Lamentations 3:45
Omnipotent *All powerful (an attribute of God)* .... Revelation 19:6
Oracle *(When referring to a place)*
  the inner sanctuary; "Holy of Holies." .... 1 Kings 6:5
Ouches *Settings for gems; sockets* .... Exodus 28:11

Outgoings *Extreme limits; furthest borders* .... Joshua 17:9
Outwent *Went before; went faster* .... Mark 6:33
Overcharged *Weighed down; burdened*................... Luke 21:34
Pangs *Extreme, sharp pains, as in childbirth*.............. Isaiah 13:8
Paps *Breasts*....................................... Ezekiel 23:21
Paramour *Male or female lover*..................... Ezekiel 23:20
Parbar *Structure on the west side of
   Solomon's temple*........................1 Chronicles 26:18
Pate *Forehead; crown of the head* .... Psalms 7:16
Patrimony *Something inherited; an estate* .... Deuteronomy 18:8
Peculiar *Particular; special; one's own*................... Exodus 19:5
Peeled *Smooth; bare; bald* .... Isaiah 18:2
Penury *Poverty* .... Proverbs 14:23
Peradventure *Perhaps* .... Genesis 18:24
Perdition *Complete loss; eternal damnation*............... John 17:12
Pernicious *Destructive, something that can injure* .... 2 Peter 2:2
Phylacteries *Scripture box attached to left arm
   or forehead by a leather strap*............. Matthew 23:5
Pilled *Pealed; stripped off skin or bark* .... Genesis 30:37-38
Pitch *A thick, dark, sticky substance* .... Genesis 6:14
Plaiting *Braiding; gathering hair into knots*................ 1 Peter 3:3
Platted *Braided; intertwined* .... Matthew 27:29
Polled his head *Cut hair from his head* .... 2 Samuel 14:26
Pommels *Bowl-shaped top of a pillar*............ 2 Chronicles 4:12-13
Post (person) *Runner; courier* .... 2 Chronicles 30:6
Potsherd *Piece of broken pottery* .... Job 2:8
Prating *Babbling; chattering* .... Proverbs 10:8, 10
Presbytery *Assembly of elders* .... 1 Timothy 4:14
Prevent *Come before, go before; anticipate* .... 2 Samuel 22:6
Pricks *OT: Thorns*................................. Num 33:55
   NT: Cattle prods or goads .... Acts 9:5

Principalities *Rulers or their territory*.................Jeremiah 13:18
Privily *In private; secretly*............................ Judges 9:31
Privy (be) *Privately knowing; knowing a secret* .... 1 Kings 2:44
Profane *Treat as common; defile* ....Leviticus 18:21
Profound (be) *Go deep into something*...................Hosea 5:2
Prognosticators *Foretellers of the future*................ Isaiah 47:13
Propitiation *Sacrifice to pay for sins against God,
    to satisfy His righteous anger*.............. Romans 3:25
Proselyte *Convert*............................. Matthew 23:15
Provender *Food for livestock or cattle*..................Genesis 24:25
Prudent *Acting with wisdom; cautious*.......1 Samuel 16:18; Isaiah 5:21
Psalm *Sacred song about or to God*..................1 Chronicles 16:7
Psaltery *Stringed instrument, as a harp or guitar* .... 1 Samuel 10:5
Publican *Tax collector*...............................Luke 5:27
Pulse *Peas, beans; legumes*......................... 2 Samuel 17:28
Purloining *Stealing; pilfering*......................... Titus 2:10
Purtenance *Inward parts; entrails*....................Exodus 12:9
Putrifying *Pertaining to gangrene; decaying*................ Isaiah 1:6
Quaternion *Guard of four soldiers* .... Acts 12:4
Quick *Alive; living* ....Leviticus 13:10
Quit *Acquitted; found not guilty*.....................Exodus 21:19
Quit you like men *Behave/act as
    a man should* .. 1 Samuel 4:9; 1 Corinthians 16:13
Raiment *Clothing; garments* ....Genesis 24:53
Rampart *Fortification; defensive structure* .... Lamentations 2:8
Rank (adj.) *Full-grown; strong and robust*.............Genesis 41:5, 7
Rase *Tear down; level; destroy* .... Psalms 137:7
Ravening *Preying upon to devour* .... Psalms 22:13
Ravin (noun) *Torn flesh; food gotten by violence*............ Nah 2:12
Ravin (verb) *Violently catch food or devour it*...........Genesis 49:27

Ravished *Raped (negative use);* ....Isaiah 13:16;
delighted (positive use) .... Proverbs 5:19
Rebuke *Reprimand; strongly warn; restrain* .... Genesis 31:42
Recompence *Punishment*
for evil, reward ..... Deuteronomy 32:35, Proverbs 12:14
Redound *Produce a result; to return* .... 2 Corinthians 4:15
Reel *Stagger, walk to and fro*
like a drunkard .... Psalms 107:27, Isaiah 24:20
Reins *Literally, kidneys.* .... Job 16:13;
Figuratively, seat of emotion .... Psalms 7:9
Remission *Forgiveness; pardon* .... Matthew 26:28
Rend *Tear apart; forcefully rip apart.* .... Exodus 39:23
Renown *Great reputation; being well-known* .... Genesis 6:4
Reproach *Disgrace; shame.* .... Genesis 30:23
Reprobate *Rejected; failing the test; lost in sin* .... Jeremiah 6:30
Reproof *Rebuke; scolding* .... Job 26:11
Requite *Repay.* .... Genesis 50:15
Rereward *Towards the rear; rear guard* .... Isaiah 52:12
Residue *Part that remains, the rest.* .... Exodus 10:5
Rie *Old spelling of "rye"; a grain.* .... Isaiah 28:25
Ringstraked *Striped, streaked.* .... Genesis 30:35 ff.
Road *Old spelling of "raid".* .... 1 Samuel 27:10
Ruddy *Reddish (hair or complexion)* .... 1 Samuel 16:12
Rude *Unskilled, unrefined or unlearned* .... 2 Corinthians 11:6
Rue *An evergreen plant used for medicine* .... Luke 11:42
Sabbath *Rest; cessation from work* .... Exodus 16:23
Sackbut *Triangular, 4-stringed instrument, like a lyre.* . Daniel 3:5, 7, 10, 15
Sacrilege *Violate or steal sacred things* .... Romans 2:22
Salutation *Greeting* .... Mark 12:38
Sanctify *Make holy; set apart for God's use.* .... Genesis 2:3
Satyr *He-goat* .... Isaiah 13:21; 34:14

Savour *Smell; taste; odor* ....Genesis 8:21
Savourest *You (singular) like; delight in; favor* .... Matthew 16:23
Scall *Scaly skin eruption*........................ Leviticus 13:30-37
Score *Multiply the number times 20 (e.g., "fourscore" = 80)* ..Genesis 16:16
Scourge *Whip; flog* ....Leviticus 19:20
Seemly *Fitting; proper; becoming*............... Proverbs 19:10; 26:1
Seethe *Boil; be very hot*............................Exodus 16:23
Selvedge *Fabric edge to prevent unraveling*................Exodus 26:4
Sepulchre *Place of burial; grave; tomb*..................Genesis 23:6
Servitor *Attendant; one performing as a servant*.......... 2 Kings 4:43
Set at nought *Despise; disregard*.................... Proverbs 1:25
Shambles *Meat market; marketplace*............. 1 Corinthians 10:25
Sheaf *Bundle of grain*................................Genesis 37:7
Sheepcote *Sheep dwelling; stable. (See "cote")* .... 1 Samuel 24:3
Sherd *See "potsherd."* .... Isaiah 30:14
Shew *Old spelling of "show."* ....Genesis 12:1
Signet *Seal or stamp, indicating the owner*..............Genesis 38:18
Single *Clear; pure; uncorrupted; healthy*................ Matthew 6:22
Sith *Old spelling of "since."* .... Ezekiel 35:6
Slack *Slow or negligent*........................Deuteronomy 7:10
Sleight *Trickery; entrapment by deceit* ....Ephesians 4:14
Slow bellies *Idle gluttons* .... Titus 1:12
Sod, sodden *Cooked; boiled*.......................Genesis 25:29
Soothsayer *One who foretells the future by ungodly means*... Joshua 13:22
Sop *A morsel of bread to be dipped*..................... John 13:26 f.
Sottish *Foolish; dull with drink; sluggish* ....Jeremiah 4:22
Spite *Anger toward someone; grief*..................... Psalms 10:14
Spoil *Booty; plunder; prey* ....Genesis 49:27
Stanched *Stopped flowing*............................Luke 8:44
Standard *Flag; banner* .... Numbers 1:52

Staves *Rods; clubs* .... Exodus 25:13

Stay him, *Support; uphold* .... Proverbs 28:17

My stay *What one relies on.* .... 2 Samuel 22:19

Stayed *Detained; held* .... Luke 4:42

Stomacher *Ornamental covering, over the chest
 and/or stomach, for females* .... Isaiah 3:24

Straightway *Right away; immediately.* .... 1 Samuel 9:13

Strait (adj.) *Narrow; close together* .... 2 Kings 6:1; Matthew 7:13

Strait (in a) *Be in distress; be in a narrow place.* .... 1 Samuel 13:6

Straitened *Impeded or restricted; narrowed* ...... Job 18:7; Ezekiel 42:6
 Distressed. .... Luke 12:50

Strake *Old spelling of "struck."* .... Acts 27:17

Strowed, strawed *Scattered; spread* .... Matthew 21:8

Succour *Help; aid.* .... Hebrew 2:18

Suffered not *Did not allow* .... Genesis 20:6

Sunder (in) *In parts; into pieces* .... Psalms 46:9

Sup *Dine; eat.* .... Luke 17:8

Sup up *Gather together; accumulate, assemble* .... Habakkuk 1:9

Superfluous *More than necessary or wanted* .... Leviticus 21:18

Suppliants *Worshippers.* .... Zephaniah 3:10

Surfeiting *Excess food or drink; overindulgence* .... Luke 21:34

Swaddling clothes *Cloths for wrapping infants tightly* ..... Luke 2:7, 12

Tablets *Small, flat ornaments or jewelry* .... Exodus 35:22

Taches *Hooks; fasteners* .... Exodus 26:6

Tale *A number; something counted* .... Exodus 5:8
 Information given; a story .... Psalms 90:9

Talent *Weight of money; weight; gift.* .... Exodus 25:39

Target *Small shield; a buckler* .... 1 Samuel 17:6

Tell *To count; number* .... Genesis 15:5

Tempered *Mixed; combined* .... Exodus 29:2

Temperance *Self-control; moderation* .... Galatians 5:23

APPENDIX

Tempest *Storm; violent wind; whirlwind*................... Job 9:17
Terrestrial *Relating to the earth; earthly*........... 1 Corinthians 15:40
Testament *A will, ratified after death; a covenant*..... Hebrews 9:16-18
Thence *From that place; from there*................... Genesis 2:10
Thereabout *About that* .... Luke 24:4
Thereat *At that place; at that* .... Exodus 30:19; Matthew 7:13
Thereby *By that; by it; as a result of that* .... Genesis 24:14; 1 Peter 2:2
Therefrom *From this; from that* .... Joshua 23:6; 2 Kings 13:2
Therein *In that; in this; in it* .... Genesis 9:7; Revelation 21:22
Thereinto *Into that* .... Luke 21:21
Thereof *Of that; of this; of it* .... Genesis 2:17; Revelation 21:23
Thereon *On that; on this; on it* ...... Genesis 35:14; Revelation 21:12
Thereout *Out of that; out of this* .... Leviticus 2:2; Judges 15:19
Thereto *To that; to this; to it* .... Exodus 25:24; Galatians 3:15
Thereunto *Unto that; unto this; unto it* ...... Exodus 32:8; 1 Peter 3:9
Thereupon *Upon that;*
        upon this; upon it .... Exodus 31:7; 1 Corinthians 3:14
Therewith *With it; with that*.................. Exodus 22:6; 30:26
Thither *To that place; opposite of hither*................ Genesis 19:20
Thitherward *Toward it; in that direction* .... Jeremiah 50:5
Thrice *Three times*................................ Exodus 34:23
Tired *Attired; put something around the head*............ 2 Kings 9:30
Tithe *The tenth part; 1/10*....................... Leviticus 27:30
Tittle *Small mark to tell between Heb. letters* . Matthew 5:18; Luke 16:17
Told out *Counted out; numbered; tallied*............. 2 Chronicles 2:2
Tow *Weaver's fiber or the yarn made from it* .... Judges 16:9
Traffick *Trade; do business*........................ Genesis 42:34
Translate *Transfer; remove to another place* .... 2 Samuel 3:10
Trodden *Walked on; trampled*................... Deuteronomy 1:36
Trode *Stepped on; walked on* .... Judges 9:27

Trow *To think; to believe; to trust* . . . . Luke 17:9
Twain *Two* . . . . 1 Samuel 18:21
Unction *An anointing.* . . . . 1 John 2:20
Unseemly *Inappropriate* . . . . Romans 1:27
Untoward *Perverse; not easily taught or guided* . . . . Acts 2:40
Usury *Interest paid for using money* . . . . Exodus 22:25
Utter court *Outer court* . . . . Ezekiel 40:31
Utter gate *Outer gate* . . . . Ezekiel 47:2
Valour *Courage; personal bravery* . . . . Joshua 1:14
Variance *Disagreement; discord; dissension* . . . . Matthew 10:35
Vaunt oneself *Boast; brag about oneself* . . . . Judges 7:2
Vehement *Violent; forceful; furious* . . . . Song of Solomon 8:6
Verily *Truly* . . . . Genesis 42:21
Verity *Truth* . . . . Psalms 111:7
Vestments *Official or ecclesiastical robes.* . . . . 2 Kings 10:22
Vesture *Garment; clothing* . . . . Deuteronomy 22:12
Victuals *Food for humans* . . . . Genesis 14:11
Villany *Extreme wickedness* . . . . Isaiah 32:6
Visage *Appearance; face; look of a person* . . . . Isaiah 52:14
Vocation *What God calls, gifts a person to do* . . . . Ephesians 4:1
Want *Lack; be deficient* . . . . Deuteronomy 28:48
Wanton *Without restraint; reckless* . . . . Isaiah 3:16
Ward *In custody, with a guard; prison.* . . . . Genesis 40:3
Wast *You (one person) were.* . . . . Genesis 3:11
Wax *Grow; become; advance.* . . . . Exodus 22:24
Wen *A wart; a tumor; a swelling* . . . . Leviticus 22:22
Wert *(If) you (one person) were* . . . . Job 8:6
Whelp *A cub; a young one.* . . . . Genesis 49:9
Whence *From what place; from where* . . . . Genesis 3:23
Whereabout *About which; concerning which* . . . . 1 Samuel 21:2

APPENDIX

Whereas *Although; when in fact* . . . . . Genesis 31:37; Deuteronomy 19:6
Whereby *By what? by which* . . . . Genesis 15:8; 1 John 2:18
Wherefore *Why? for which reason* . . . . . . Genesis 10:9; Revelation 17:7
Wherein *In which; in what* . . . . Genesis 1:30; Revelation 18:19
Whereinsoever *In whatever thing* . . . . 2 Corinthians 11:21
Whereinto *Into which* . . . . Leviticus 11:33; John 6:22
Whereof *Of which; of what* . . . . Genesis 3:11; 1 John 4:3
Whereon *On which; on what* . . . . Genesis 28:13; John 4:38
Whereto *To what? to which* . . . . Job 30:2; Philippians 3:16
Whereunto *Unto what; unto which* . . . . Numbers 36:3; 2 Peter 1:19
Whereupon *Upon which;*
          for which reason . . . . Leviticus 11:35; Hebrews 9:18
Wherewith *With which; with what?* . . . . Genesis 27:41; Mark 9:50
Wherewithal *How? with what?* . . . . Psalms 119:9; Matthew 6:31
Whether is? *Which of the two?* . . . . Judges 9:2
Whither *To what place; to where* . . . . Genesis 16:8
Wimples *Curled hair; veils crimped* . . . . Isaiah 3:22
Winefat *Wine vat* . . . . Isaiah 63:2
Wines on the lees *Wines fermented on their dregs* . . . . Isaiah 25:6
Wist, wot *Knew; thought; supposed* . . . . Exodus 16:15
Withal *With it/them; with;*
          at the same time . . . . Exodus 25:29; 1 Timothy 5:13
Withs *Twigs twisted to make a band, rope* . . . . Judges 16:7-9
Wont *Used to; in the habit of* . . . . Exodus 21:29

Hebrew Calendar

The Hebrew Calendar is based upon the lunar cycle of 29.5 days. Each month begins with the new moon. For example, Abib/Nisan will be 29.5 days somewhere within Gregorian March and April.

Month#	Bible Name	Additional Information
1st	Abib, Nisan	7th Month (Gen)* March-April** Current Name: **Nisan**
2nd	Zif	8th Month (Gen)* April-May** Current Name: **Iyar**
3rd	Sivan	9th Month (Gen)* May-June** Current Name: **Sivan**
4th	(no name)	10th Month (Gen)* June-July** Current Name: **Tammuz**
5th	(no name)	11th Month (Gen)* July-August** Current Name: **Av**
6th	Elul	12th Month (Gen)* August-Sept.** Current Name: **Elul**
7th	Ethanim	1st Month (Gen)* Sept.-Oct.** Current Name: **Tishri**
8th	Bul	2nd Month (Gen)* Oct.-Nov.** Current Name: **Marcheshvan or Cheshvan**
9th	Chisleu	3rd Month (Gen)* Nov.-Dec.** Current Name: **Kislev**
10th	Tebeth	4th Month (Gen)* Dec.-Jan.** Current Name: **Tevet**
11th	Sebat	5th Month (Gen)* Jan.-Feb.** Current Name: **Shevat**
12th	Adar	6th Month (Gen)* Feb.-Mar.** Current Name: **Adar**

* Old calendar used in Genesis
** Gregorian Calendar

APPENDIX

In Exodus 12:2, God told Moses that the month of the Exodus would be "the beginning of months." From that time forward, the Hebrews had a new (post-Exodus) calendar, with the year starting in Abib.

Where names are used in the Bible
1st month: Ex. 12:2; 2 Ki. 29:17; Eze. 29:17; 30:20; 45:18, 21 **Abib:** Ex. 13:4; 23:15; 34:18; Dt. 16:1; **Nisan:** Neh. 2:1; Est. 3:7 **Beginning of the year:** Eze. 40:1
Zif: 1 Ki. 6:1, 37
3rd month: Ex. 19:1; Eze. 31:1 **Sivan:** Est. 8:9
4th month: Jer. 39:2; 52:6; Eze. 1:1
5th month: 2 Ki. 25:8; Jer. 52:12; Eze. 20:1
Elul: Neh. 6:15; Eze. 8:1; Hag.1:1
1st month: Gen. 8:13 **7th month:** Lev. 16:29; 23:24, 32; Num. 29:1; Eze. 45:25; Hag. 2:1 **Ethanim:** 1 Ki. 8:2
2nd month: Gen. 7:11 **Bul:** 1 Ki. 6:38 **8th month:** 1 Ki. 12:32, 33
Chisleu: Neh. 1:1 **9th month:** Ezr. 10:9
Tebeth: Est. 2:16 **10th month:** 2 Ki. 25:1; Jer. 52:4; Eze. 24:1; 29:1; 33:21
11th month: Dt. 1:3 **Sebat:** Zec. 1:7
Adar: Ezr.6:15; Est. 3:7, 13; 8:12; 9:1, 15, 17, 19, 21 **12th month:** 2 Ki. 25:27; Jer. 52:31; Eze. 32:1

Hebrew Feast Days

Feast Day(s)	Time of year
Passover	Nisan 14 (Mar-April)
Feast of Unleavened Bread	Nisan 15-21 (Mar-April)
Feast of Weeks / Harvest / Pentecost	Sivan 6 (May-Jun): 7 weeks after Passover
Feast of Trumpets (Rosh Hashanah)	Tishri 1 (Sept-Oct)
Day of Atonement (Yom Kippur)	Tishri 10 (Sept-Oct)
Feast of Tabernacles (Sukkoth)	Tishri 15-21 (Sept-Oct)
Feast of Dedication (Hanukkah)	Kislev 25-30 (Nov-Dec) & Tevet 1-2 (Dec-Jan)
Feast of Purim	Adar (Feb-Mar) 14

APPENDIX

Where names are used in the Bible
Passover: Lev. 23:5; Nu. 9:5; 28:16; 33:3; Dt. 16:1-6; Jos. 5:10-11; 2 Ch. 35:1; Ezr. 6:9; Mt. 26:2, etc.
Feast of unleavened bread: Ex. 12:17; 23:15; 34:18; Lev. 23:6; Nu. 28:17; Dt. 16:16; 2 Ch. 8:13; 35:17; Ezr. 6:22, etc.
Feast of weeks: Ex. 34:22; Dt. 16:10, 16; 2 Ch. 8:13 **Feast of harvest:** Ex. 23:16 **Pentecost:** Ac. 2:1; 20:16; 1 Co. 16:8
A sabbath / a memorial of blowing of trumpets / an holy convocation: Lev. 23:24; Nu. 29:1
Day of atonement: Lev. 23:27-28; 25:9. See also Ex. 30:10.
Feast of tabernacles: Lev. 23:34; Dt. 16:13, 16; 31:10; 2 Ch. 8:13; Ezr. 3:4; Hos. 12:9; Zec. 14:16-19; Jn. 7:2 **Feast of ingathering:** Ex. 23:16; 34:22
Feast of the dedication: Jn. 10:22
(Days of) Purim: Est. 9:26, 28-29, 31-32

Hebrew Time

The Hebrews' day began at sunset. It grouped the daylight and night hours into 3-hour watches.

Time of day/night	Clock time	Names used in the Bible
Sunset		**Sun set(ting):** Gen. 28:11; Mk. 1:32; Lk. 4:40 **The even:** Lev. 11:24-40; Mt. 8:16, etc. **Evening:** Gen. 8:11; 24:11, etc.
First watch: Sunset to 9pm		
1st hour	Sunset - 7pm	
2nd hour	7 - 8pm	
3rd hour	8 - 9pm	**3rd hour of the night:** Acts. 23:23
Second watch: 9 - 12pm		**2nd watch:** Lk. 12:38
4th hour	9 - 10pm	
5th hour	10 - 11pm	
6th hour	11pm - 12am	
Midnight At the 6th hour	About 12am	**Midnight:** Ex. 11:4; 12:29; Jdg. 16:3; Ru. 3:8; 1 Ki. 3:20; Job 34:20; Ps. 119:62; Mt. 25:6; Mk. 13:35; Lk. 11:5; Ac. 16:25; 20:7; 27:27
Third watch: 12 - 3am		**Third watch:** Lk. 12:38
7th hour	12 - 1am	
8th hour	1 - 2am	
9th hour	2 - 3am	
Fourth watch: 3am - 6am		**Cockcrowing:** Mk. 13:35 **Fourth watch of the night:** Mt. 14:25; Mk. 6:48
10th hour	3 - 4am	
11th hour	4 - 5am	
12th hour	5 - Sunrise	

APPENDIX

Time of day/night	Clock time	Names used in the Bible
Sunrise	About 6am	**Day break/break of day:** Gen. 32:24, 26; 2 Sa. 2:32; Song 2:17; 4:6; Ac. 20:11
First watch: 6am - 9am		
1st hour	Sunrise - 7am	
2nd hour	7 - 8am	
3rd hour	8 - 9am	**3rd hour:** Mt. 20:3; Mk. 15:25; Ac. 2:15
Second watch: 9am - 12pm		
4th hour	9 - 10am	
5th hour	10 - 11am	
6th hour	11 - Noon	**6th hour:** Mt. 20:5; 27:45; Mk. 15:33; Lk. 23:44; Jn. 4:6; 19:14; Ac. 10:9
Noon		**Noonday:** Dt. 28:29; Job 5:14; Job 11:17; Ps. 37:6; 91:6; Isa. 16:3; 58:10; 59:10; Jer. 15:8 **Midday:** 1Ki. 18:29; Neh. 8:3; Acts 26:13
Third watch: 12 - 3pm		
7th hour	Noon - 1pm	**7th hour:** Jn. 4:52
8th hour	1 - 2pm	
9th hour	2 - 3pm	**9th hour:** Mt. 20:5; 27:45-46; Mk. 15:33-34; Lk. 23:44; Ac. 3:1; 10:3, 30
Fourth watch: 3 - 6pm		
10th hour	3 - 4pm	**10th hour:** Jn. 1:39
11th hour	4 - 5pm	**11th hour:** Mt. 20:6, 9
12th hour	5 - Sunset	

HEBREW WEIGHTS

Weight	Hebrew / Greek	Ratio to a shekel
Talent (OT)	Kikkar	3,000 shekels
Talent (NT)	Talanton	2,320 – 3,200 shekels
Maneh / Pound	Maneh (Heb) / Mna (Gk)	50 shekels
Pound (of ointment)	Litra (Gk. from Latin)	30 shekels
Shekel	Shekel	1 shekel (20 gerahs)
Bekah	Bekah	1/2 shekel
Gerah	Gerah	1/20 shekel

APPENDIX

Weight (US)	Weight (Metric)	Names used in the Bible
75 lbs.	34.2 kg.	**Talent:** Ex. 25:39; 37:24; 38:27; 2 Sa. 12:30; 1 Ki. 20:39; 2 Ki 5:22; 23:33; 1 Ch. 20:2; 36:3; Zec. 5:7
58-80 lbs.	26.3-36.3 kg.	**Talent:** Mt. 25:24, 25, 28; Rev. 16:21
1.25 lbs.	.57 kg.	**Maneh:** Eze. 45:12 **Pound:** 1 Ki. 10:17; Ezr. 2:69; Neh. 7:71-72; Lu. 19:13, 16, 18, 20, 24-25
12 oz	.34 kg	**Pound:** John 12:3; 19:39
.4 oz.	11.4 gr.	**Shekel:** Gen. 23:15-16; 24:22; Ex. 30:13
.2 oz	5.7 gr.	**Bekah:** Ex. 38:26 (otherwise called **half a shekel:** Gen. 24:22; 30:13; etc.)
.02 oz	.57 gr.	**Gerah:** Ex. 30:13; Lev. 27:25; Num. 3:47; 18:16; Eze. 45:12

BIBLICAL MONEY

The value depended upon two elements: the weight of the coins; and whether they were silver or gold. The scripture verses for these coins are the same as above in the Hebrew Weights section.

Hebrew Coins	Amount
Talent	60 minahs, 3,000 shekels
Maneh, Pound (mna)	50 shekels
Shekel	1 shekel

Roman Coins	Amount & Days' Wage	Scriptures
Penny (silver denarion)	1 denarius = 1 day's wage	Mt. 20:2, 9-10, 13; 22:19; Mk. 12:15; Lk. 20:24; Rev. 6:6
Farthing (copper assarion)	1/16 denarius	Mt. 10:29; Lk. 12:6
Farthing (bronze kodrantes)	1/4 assarius = 1/64 denarius = 2 Greek mites	Mt. 5:26; Mk. 12:42

Greek Coins	Amount & Days' Wage	Scriptures
Piece of money (Stater, tetradrachma)	4 drachmas	Mt. 17:27
Tribute money (didrachma)	2 drachmas	Mt. 17:24
Piece of silver (drachma)	1 drachma = 1 day's wage	Luke 15:8-9
Mite (Lepton)	1/8 drachma = 1/2 farthing (kodrantes) = 1/128 drachma	Mk. 12:42; Lk. 12:59; 21:2

APPENDIX

Biblical Measures

Note: All measures are approximate. Modern measures are much more precise.

Length

Unit	Comparison	Scriptures
Roman mile (milion Gk)	8 furlongs (stadia) or 4,858 feet.	Mt. 5:41
Sabbath day's journey	2,000 cubits	Ac. 1:12
Furlong (stadion Gk)	About 200 yards or 607.25 feet	Lk. 24:13; Jn. 6:19; 11:18; 1 Co. 9:24; Rev. 14:20; 21:16
Reed (kalamos Gk)	6 cubits (Heb) or 10 feet (Gk, Rom)	Re. 11:1; 21:15-16
Fathom (orguia Gk)	2 paces or 6 feet	Ac. 27:28
Pace	2 cubits or 3 feet	(Not in scripture)
Cubit (ammah, gomed Heb; pechys Gk)	18 inches (standard) 21 inches (Ezekiel's temple)	Ge. 6:15-16, and 250 other verses Eze. 43:13 and throughout ch. 40-47
Span (zereth Heb)	9 inches	Ex. 28:16; 39:9; 1 Sa. 17:4; La. 2:20; Eze. 43:13
Handbreadth (tophach Heb)	4 fingers or 3 inches	Ex. 25:25; 37:12; Eze. 40:5, 43; 43:13
Finger	.75 inch	(Not in scripture)

Dry Measure

Unit	Comparison	Scriptures
Cor (kor Heb)	1 homer or 10 ephahs or 6.52 bushels. A vessel that held 1 homer could hold 10 baths (liquid)	Only used as liquid in Eze. 45:14
Homer (chomer Heb)	1 homer or 10 ephahs or 6.52 bushels. A vessel that held 1 homer could hold 10 baths (liquid)	Lev. 27:16; Is. 5:10; Eze. 45:10, 13-14; Hos. 3:2
Half homer (lethech Heb)	5 ephahs or 3.26 bushels	Hos. 3:2
Ephah (Heb)	1/10 homer or .65 bushel or 20.8 quarts	Ex. 16:36; Le. 19:36; Ru. 2:17; Eze. 45:11; etc.
Bushel (modios Gk)	7.68 quarts	Mt. 5:15; Mk. 4:21; Lk. 11:33
Measure (seah Heb)	1/3 ephah or 7 quarts	Gen. 18:6; 1 Sa. 25:18; 1 Ki. 18:32; 2 Ki. 7:1, 16, 18
Omer (omer Heb)	1/10 ephah or 2.08 quarts or 1 4/5 (1.8) cabs	Ex. 16:16, 18, 22, 32-33, 36

Liquid Measure

Unit	Comparison	Scriptures
Cor (kor Heb)	10 baths or 60 gallons or the amount of liquid inside a vessel that could hold a homer (dry).	Eze. 45:14
Firkin (metretes Gk)	Estimates vary from 7-10 gallons.	Jn. 2:6
Bath	1/10 cor or 6 hins or 6 gallons. 10 baths (liquid) could fit in a vessel that held 1 cor (liquid) or 1 homer (dry).	Isa. 5:10; Eze. 45:10-11, 14
Hin	1/6 bath or 1 gallon or 2 cabs	Ex. 29:40; 30:24; Lev. 19:36; 23:13; Nu. 15:4-7, 9-10; 28:5, 7, 14; Eze. 4:11; 45:24; 46:5, 7, 11, 14
Cab (kab Heb)	4 logs or 1.16 quarts	2 Ki. 6:25
Log	¼ cab or .29 quarts or .58 pint	Lev. 14:10, 12, 15, 21, 24

The Bible's Internal Timeline

God is a God of history. His prophets prophesy and then God fulfills the words He spoke through them. Then we can fit them on a timeline. God makes Himself known through history.

It turns out that God made an interlocking chain of events, all the way from Genesis 5:3 at the genealogy of Adam, through to the laying of the temple's foundation in 1 Kings 6:1.

It is amazing. Not only does it take us from one date to the next, it also links us from event to event, often many chapters over from the previous date in the chain. Once we have this chain set, or written in our Bibles, it dates other events that occur between the dates that we already have.

For instance, if we know how old Abraham and Sarah were when God and the two angels appeared to them, and their age when Isaac was born, we know within a year when Sodom and Gomorrah were destroyed.

This timeline is no-frills. It simply gives the date, the event(s), the character(s) and the scripture where it says so. Then if the chain is not continued in the next verse, it indicates which next verse continues the unbroken chain, so you don't get lost in the intermediate dates and events. This way you can mark your Bible to tell where the next date in the chain is.

Year AM*	Year BC**	Event	Scripture(s)	Generation
0	4114	Creation of **Adam**	Gen 5:1	1
130	3984	Adam (130) begat **Seth**	Gen 5:3	2

*Anno Mundi = The year of the world   **Before Christ

APPENDIX

Year AM*	Year BC**	Event	Scripture(s)	Generation
235	3879	Seth (105) begat **Enosh**	Gen 5:6	3
325	3781	Enosh (90) begat **Cainan**	Gen 5:9	4
395	3719	Cainan (70) begat **Mahalaleel**	Gen 5:12	5
460	3654	Mahalaleel (65) begat **Jared**	Gen 5:15	6
622	3476	Jared (162) begat **Enoch**	Gen 5:18	7
687	3427	Enoch begat **Methuselah**	Gen 5:21	8
874	3240	Methuselah begat **Lamech**	Gen 5:25	9
987	3127	Enoch (at 365) was not; for God took him	Gen 5:23-4	8
1056	3058	Lamech begat **Noah**	Gen 5:28-9	10
1536	2578	120 years decreed for man	Gen 6:2-3	
1556	2558	Noah (500) begat **Shem**, Ham, and Japheth (Go to Gen 11:10)	Gen 5:32, Gen 6:10	11
1656	2458	God flooded the entire earth	Gen 7:6	
1658	2456	Shem (100) begat **Arphaxad**, 2 yrs after the flood (From Gen 5:32)	Gen 11:10	12
1693	2421	Arphaxad (35) begat **Salah**	Gen 11:12	13
1723	2391	Salah (30) begat **Eber**	Gen 11:14	14
1757	2357	Eber (34) begat **Peleg**	Gen 11:16	15

*Anno Mundi = The year of the world   **Before Christ

Year AM*	Year BC**	Event	Scripture(s)	Generation
1787	2327	Peleg (30) begat **Reu**	Gen 11:18	16
1819	2295	Reu (32) begat **Serug**	Gen 11:20	17
1849	2265	Serug (30) begat **Nahor**	Gen 11:22	18
1878	2236	Nahor (29) begat **Terah**	Gen 11:24	19
1948	2166	Terah (70) begat **Abram**, Nahor, and Haran (Go to Gen 21:5 for Isaac)	Gen 11:26	20
2023	2091	Abram (75) departed from Haran	Gen 12:4	20
2034	2080	Abram (86) begat Ishmael by Hagar	Gen 16:16	21
2047	2067	The Lord appeared to Abram (99)	Gen 17:1	21
2047	2067	Abram (99) and Ishmael (13) are both circumcised	Gen 17:24-5	
2047 or 2048	2067 or 2066	Sodom and Gomorrah destroyed	Gen 19	
2048	2066	Sarah will be 90 when Abraham is 100. Sarah is 10 years younger.	Gen 17:17	
2048	2066	Abraham (100) begat **Isaac** by Sarah	Gen 21:3-5	21
2085	2029	Sarah (127) died; Abraham (137)	Gen 23:1	

*Anno Mundi = The year of the world   **Before Christ

APPENDIX

Year AM*	Year BC**	Event	Scripture(s)	Generation
2088	2026	Isaac (40) married Rebekah	Gen 25:20	21
2108	2006	Isaac (60) begat **Jacob** and Esau (Go to Gen 45)	Gen 25:24-6	22
2123	1991	Abraham (175) died	Gen 25:7	20
2148	1966	Esau (40) married Judith and Basemath (Hittites)	Gen 26:34	22
2171	1943	Ishmael (137) died	Gen 25:17	21
2200	1914	Jacob begat **Joseph** (see note at 2238/1876)	Gen 30:24	23
2217	1897	Joseph (17) when sold to Potiphar	Gen 37:2	
2228	1886	Isaac (180) died	Gen 35:28	21
2228	1886	Joseph (28) interpreted the butler and baker's dreams	Gen 40	
2230	1884	Joseph (30) stood before Pharaoh	Gen 41:1, 46	
2238	1876	Jacob (130) with 5 yrs of famine left. So 7 yrs plenty: 2230/1884 - 2236/1878. 7 yrs famine: 2237/1873 - 2243/1871. Joseph (30) before 7 yrs plenty, 2230/1884 (41:46). So Joseph born 2200/1914.	Gen 45:11; 47:9	
2238	1876	**The year Israel (Jacob) came to Egypt**	Gen 45-47:10	

*Anno Mundi = The year of the world **Before Christ

Year AM*	Year BC**	Event	Scripture(s)	Generation
2255	1859	Jacob (147) died (Joseph was 55)	Gen 47:28	22
2310	1804	Joseph (110) died	Gen 50:26	23
2558	1526	Amram begat Moses by Jochebed	Ex 2:1-10; 6:20	
2628	1486	Moses (40) fled from Pharaoh into Midian	Ex 2:11; Acts 7:30	
2668	1446	Moses (80) encountered God at the burning bush after 40 yrs in Midian	Acts 7:30; Ex 3-4	
2668	1446	**Israel sojourned in Egypt 430 years until Exodus**	Ex 12:40	
2708	1406	Moses (120) died, after 40 years in the wilderness. So 80 at Exodus, 40 when he fled Pharaoh (Acts 7:30), born 2588/1526.	Dt 31:2; 34:7	
3074	1040	**David** born	2 Sam 5:4	33
3104	1010	David (30) began to reign	2 Sam 5:4	33
3144	970	David (70) reigned 40 yrs, then **Solomon**	1 Kgs 2:11-12	34

*Anno Mundi = The year of the world   **Before Christ

APPENDIX

Year AM*	Year BC**	Event	Scripture(s)	Generation
3148	966	Temple begun **480 yrs after Exodus**, in 4th yr of Solomon's reign. **Solomon began his reign in 970, based on secular and other dates. This date is the basis for all other dates back to Creation, which would be 4114 BC.**	1 Kgs 6:1	
3144-3184	970-930	Solomon reigned over Israel 40 years	1 Kgs 11:42; 2 Chr 9:30	34

*Anno Mundi = The year of the world   **Before Christ

ALSO BY DAVID W. DANIELS

Available from Chick Publications

LOOK WHAT'S MISSING

For years, publishers have been removing words, and even whole verses, from modern Bibles. What's missing from your Bible?

ANSWERS TO YOUR BIBLE VERSION QUESTIONS

David W. Daniels answers difficult questions about the KJV. Learn how to defend the KJV and why you can trust it.

DID THE CATHOLIC CHURCH GIVE US THE BIBLE?

The Bible has two histories. One is of God preserving His words through His people. The other is of the devil using Roman Catholic "scholars" to pervert God's words and give us corrupt modern Bibles.

WHY THEY CHANGED THE BIBLE

See who is behind the gradual changing of modern Bibles. There's no guessing about what these people believe. They will tell you, in their own words!

BUT I TRUST THE SCHOLARS

There are two kinds of Bible scholars: the scholars of faith and the scholars of doubt. Which one will YOU trust?

IS THE "WORLD'S OLDEST BIBLE" A FAKE?

Here is proof that the Sinaiticus, a supposedly ancient Bible text on which modern Bibles are based, is actually a 19th century fake.

51 REASONS WHY THE KING JAMES

Here are 51 reasons to trust that God kept His promise to preserve His own words.

ALSO BY DAVID W. DANIELS

Available from Chick Publications

KING JAMES BIBLE COMPANION

Definitions of over 600 less-familiar KJV words. Tuck it in your King James Bible as a handy reference tool

CAN YOU TRUST JUST ONE BIBLE?

Answers to the most common anti-KJV accusations.

DID JESUS USE THE SEPTUAGINT?

They're saying Jesus used the Septuagint. But what they really want is to add something to your Bible.

BABYLON RELIGION

Learn how a Babylonian goddess became the Virgin Mary. An easy-to-read history of Catholicism's Babylonian origin.

HOT TOPICS

Over the years, Jack Chick has written some tracts on such "politically incorrect" issues that Christians were often afraid to pass them out. Yet those messages are both current and biblical.

SHOULD A CHRISTIAN BE A MASON?

Well-known masons, in their own words, show why no Christian should be a Mason.

YOU DON'T KNOW JACK

The authorized biography of Christian cartoonist, Jack T. Chick.

Printed in Dunstable, United Kingdom